FUNDAMENTALS OF CATHOLICISM

FUNDAMENTALS

OF

CATHOLICISM

by

KENNETH BAKER, S.J.

IGNATIUS PRESS   SAN FRANCISCO

Imprimi Potest: Thomas R. Royce, S.J.
Provincial, Oregon Province
of the Society of Jesus
Portland, Oregon

Imprimatur: + Thomas J. Welsh
Bishop of Arlington, Virginia

Cover design by Riz Boncan Marsella

Fifth printing, 1995
© 1982 Kenneth Baker, S.J.
ISBN 0-89870-017-5
Library of Congress catalogue number 82-80297
Co-published by Ignatius Press, San Francisco
and Homiletic & Pastoral Review
86 Riverside Drive, New York, N.Y. 10024
Printed in the United States of America

CONTENTS

Part II: THE COMMANDMENTS

PREFACE

"Confusion" is an apt word to describe the intellectual climate of our time. This is true, in my view, not only of Western culture in general, but also of the thinking of very many Catholics—in Europe, in North America and in South America.

While teaching a college course a few years ago on the fundamentals of the Catholic faith to about forty students, I came to the realization that over ninety percent of them did not understand the most basic tenets of their Catholic faith. Subsequently I suggested in a few short articles that we needed something like "Remedial Catholicism" in our colleges and universities, just as we offer remedial courses in English and mathematics.

Gradually I came to the realization that there should be more teaching and preaching about the basics of Catholicism. About that time Charles W. Carruth, editor of the *Arlington Catholic Herald*, Arlington, Virginia, asked me to begin writing a series of columns for the diocesan newspaper. First, I secured permission from *Twin Circle* to reprint a series on the Creed that I had written a few years before. When they were almost exhausted, I decided to complement them with a series on the moral teachings of the Church by taking each of the Ten Commandments. Those articles compose Volume I of this series.

After completing the series on the Ten Commandments, it seemed to me good to work my way through the entire body of doctrinal teaching of the Catholic faith. Those articles, which appeared in the *Herald* over a period of about four years, cover the following doctrinal areas: in Volume II you will find the treatment of God, Trinity, Creation, Christ and Mary; in Volume III you will find the treatment of Grace, Church, Seven Sacraments and Eschatology or the Last Things.

What I have tried to do in these short articles is to present faithfully the traditional Catholic teaching on all the important points of doctrine and morals.

Who were these articles written for? They were written primarily for ordinary Catholic lay men and women who are looking for some direction in the present sea of confusion, and who would like to know more about the Catholic faith that they profess. I have covered all the basic "theses" of Catholic theology and have tried to express them in non-technical language, as far as this was possible.

The original purpose of the articles, therefore, was to help concerned Catholics reach a deeper understanding of their faith. But it seems to me that they could rightly be given to non-Catholics who are seriously interested in Catholicism. These volumes can help the non-Catholic understand the Catholic faith better—and perhaps even come to embrace it. Also, because of the nature of the short essays, they might be used by priests as the basis of simple sermons on the essentials of the faith.

These articles did not just come out of my head. They are based on the traditional treatises of theology that all priests study in the seminary. I am indebted, therefore, to my professors in the seminary and to many books that I have consulted in the course of writing these essays. The books that I have relied on primarily for guidance are the following:

Holy Bible
Enchiridion Symbolorum, Denzinger-Schoenmetzer

Fundamentals of Catholic Dogma, Ludwig Ott
Summa Theologica, Thomas Aquinas
Summa Contra Gentiles, Thomas Aquinas
New Catholic Encyclopedia
The Catholic Catechism, John A. Hardon, S.J.
The Teaching of Christ, Ronald Lawler *et al.*
Dictionary of Theology, Louis Bouyer
Documents of Vatican II, Walter M. Abbott, S.J., Editor

I wish to thank first of all Charles W. Carruth for his help and encouragement. It was due to him that all of these articles appeared in the *Arlington Catholic Herald* as a weekly column, beginning in January 1976. My thanks go also in a special way to Most Reverend Thomas J. Welsh, Bishop of Arlington, who read the articles in his own newspaper and kindly consented to write the Introduction to these volumes. Finally, I want to thank Fr. Joseph Fessio, S.J., and his devoted collaborators at Ignatius Press for their diligence and patience in the production of these three volumes.

It is my earnest hope and prayer that these short essays on the fundamentals of Catholic faith will assist many —both Catholics and non-Catholics—to acquire a better understanding of the inexhaustible treasure of Catholic truth. With the help of God's grace, understanding should lead to love, love to acceptance, and acceptance to fearless Christian living in our "age of confusion". For, nothing is more effective in rooting out the darkness of error and confusion than the brilliant white light of Catholic truth.

October 15, 1981   KENNETH BAKER, S.J.
Feast of St. Teresa of Avila
New York, N.Y.

INTRODUCTION

Pilgrims to the Shrine of Lourdes in France close their day of prayer with a torchlight procession that begins near the Grotto and winds along the walkways to circle back and end in front of the Basilica. All the while in languages from around the world they sing over and over again the Lourdes Hymn, this group or that one, leading the verses in French or Italian or Polish and everyone joining in the refrain. When, finally, all are close together in front of the church, they chant in Latin the Gregorian Creed. It is an inspirational moment that reminds all present of their one faith. I thank Fr. Kenneth Baker for beginning this three-volume work by a beautiful series of articles on the Creed. They reminded me of that faith experience at Lourdes and pointed up the special quality of his writing.

"To know, love and serve God." That was a simple and easily memorized formula of yesteryear. This work of Fr. Baker speaks in the same arresting simplicity and rewards the persistent prober in the same way.

If one asks the question: is there need today for a straightforward series on the fundamentals of faith, an easy answer would be that there must be since Pope John Paul II has been so often busy about that very thing. When he visited the United States in October 1979 he spoke to the bishops at length about fundamentals. He congratulated them on their teachings in defense of life, on indissolubility of marriage, on celibacy, on morality. His encyclicals have stressed the fundamentals that Christ is the Redeemer of mankind and that God is rich in mercy. His message in Mexico was that there can be no real approach to the solution of the problems of mankind unless we first understand who God is. Everywhere the large "M" for Mary on his coat of arms points to him kneeling in prayer at Mary's shrine in Czestochowa, Knock, Loreto and Guadalupe. Only a would-be assassin's bullets kept him from Lourdes. He knows that the law of praying and the law of faith are one. His fundamental prayer literally around the world has been to Mary, Mother of God and Mother of the Church.

But let us not approach the question backwards: there is not a need to stress fundamentals because the Pope is doing it. Rather, the Vicar of Christ is doing it because there is the need!

Some will surely say that these volumes are not for them because they received a good Catholic education, know their faith and have no special need for a simple review. For such we might point out that "fundamental" and "simple" do not mean quite the same thing. These volumes contain series of articles stating and explaining the key doctrines of our Catholic faith. They are clear and precise but not by any means on a grade school level. They are built on the Scriptures, as is our faith, but addressed to mankind on the threshold of the twenty-first century as was Vatican II. Indeed the reading of several chapters will convince most people that their memories are not quite as sharp as they believed and that new insights on old truths are a special delight.

That point perhaps bears elaboration: even if we had a good Catholic education, profited from it and retained a lot of it, the passage of time and the changing circumstances in the world and in our lives make a review of our faith quite rewarding. We are not the people we were ten, twenty or thirty years ago at age eighteen. The old devil has produced some new challenges to the old faith. It is only when many of our loved ones have died that we learn we really need to believe in "the resurrection of the body and life everlasting".

Some would say that our promotion of these volumes sounds like a "save the saved" campaign. Let us first respond with a word in defense of the needs of good people that they might become better since the Lord has called us to the challenge of becoming perfect as is the heavenly Father, and since today too many good things such as indissolubility in marriage or virginity outside of marriage are passed over as ideals, that is, impossible.

But then let us note and strongly that this work has even greater value for the unsure and for the uninformed or misinformed. It is at once the challenge and the beauty of our faith that we must have some grasp of all of it to appreciate and sometimes even accept some of its parts. Challenges to the Church's teaching on sexual morality are defeated finally in the arena of our understanding of the Church as being divinely instituted and just as divinely safeguarded in this twentieth century. The man or woman face to face with crushing suffering, loneliness or disappointment and asking "how can a good God. . . ?" will find no better answer than the mystery of sinless Mary at the foot of the Cross giving up her Son and receiving us, his executioners, in exchange.

Fr. Baker's ability to state the truth clearly and yet with insightful newness may remind some of Frank Sheed or G. K. Chesterton. It will jolt some others free of errors firmly clutched and slip a ray of hope into some hearts all but tightly shuttered against the eternal light.

15

It is most especially for this last quality that I encourage the reading of these volumes. Fr. Baker, at the end of the first volume, puts it this way: "It is one thing to be able to recite the Nicene Creed with understanding at Sunday Mass; it is something else to live our Catholic lives in the full realization and implementation of the Creed. In these short essays I have tried to convey more knowledge about the essentials of our Catholic faith. Knowledge is not the same thing as faith, but it is an essential part of it. Our Lord Himself said: 'This is eternal life: to know you, the only true God, and Jesus Christ whom you have sent' (Jn 17:3)."

On almost every page the Catholic faith of the author comes through. It is second nature for him to offer applications of the truth to situations in the lives of young and old, applications so real and present as to force the reader to turn from the truth on the written pages to the need for it in his or her own life.

The great Pope Paul VI in his Exhortation on Evangelization, his last and perhaps greatest legacy, reminds us that the question in evangelization is not whether or not people can be saved without our preaching to them —surely they can by the merciful God—but whether *we can be saved* without spreading the Good News! An effect of these volumes will be to arm the reader with more truth, and like Jeremiah he will be unable to contain it. The truth of Christ impels us to share him with non-Christians. The beauty of the seven sacraments, I stress *seven*, will make us want to share all of them with our Protestant friends or family members. Mary, Mother of the Church, will encourage all of us to seek her intercession that we may all be one. We do believe Christ will come again. We do believe in everlasting life. It is only for lack of thinking about it that we are not doing that which Christ has left undone in filling the many mansions in our Father's house. Fr. Baker starts us thinking and acting!

July 31, 1981
Feast of St. Ignatius

+THOMAS J. WELSH
BISHOP OF
ARLINGTON, VIRGINIA

PART I

THE CREED

FAITH AND THE GOOD NEWS

Given the massive confusion today in religious questions, even the most fundamental ones such as the existence of God, the immortality of the human soul, the
possibility of faith and the divinity of Our Lord Jesus
Christ, it can be very helpful to reflect on the basic tenets
of our Catholic faith.

Since practically every article of the Nicene Creed—
which we profess at Mass every Sunday—has been called
into question and put in doubt in recent years by some
theologians and intellectuals, I have thought it best to
begin this series with a number of articles on the Creed.

Let us start with the Catholic notion of faith. At every
Sunday Mass, before we step forward to receive the
Body and Blood of Christ in Holy Communion, the
Church bids us confess our faith in the Triune God by
praying the Apostles' Creed. We commence with the
momentous words that proclaim to all men that we are
believing Christians, "We believe in one God." What is
this faith that makes us Christians or followers of Christ?
First of all, we must realize that faith is a supernatural gift
from God. Before a person can believe he must receive
the grace of God—and God's grace is the free gift of
himself to man. Our Lord himself says in John (6:44),
"No one can come to me unless my Father draws him."
This applies to the first stirrings of faith in the pagan as
well as to the advanced sanctity of the saints and the
Blessed Virgin Mary.

Secondly, faith is both a subjective, interior act of the mind and will of the believing person and also the objective content of what is believed. Thus, when we say that Jane has the faith, we mean that interiorly she accepts God's revelation about himself that he has made known to her through his Church. This faith gives her security about God's love for her. It gives her confidence and hope for the future. It fills her heart with love for the God who gives himself to man. In this sense we are talking about Jane's interior state of mind.

But the word "faith" also refers to the *content*, or what is believed. According to St. Paul, faith, in addition to being a gift from God, also proceeds from the preaching of the Apostles and those sent by them. Here I would urge you to pick up your family Bible and read chapters 2 and 3 of the Acts of the Apostles. There you will find a brief, complete outline of Christian faith in the objective sense. The faith preached by the Apostles comes to this:

God the Father sent his own Son Jesus into the world to save mankind from sin and death as the prophets long ago foretold. Jesus was a good man who went about curing the sick but the Jewish authorities rejected him and put him to death. God raised him up on the third day and we are all witnesses to his resurrection. Therefore repent of your sins, believe this Good News, be baptized and you will be saved from the power of the devil.

Scripture tells us that after St. Peter preached the first Christian sermon on the first Pentecost, three thousand people became believers and were baptized. From that moment they became "new creatures" because they were freed from sin and immersed in the knowledge and love of the living God.

SUBMISSION TO GOD

Every article of the Creed has been attacked by someone in recent years. The man or woman of faith who can live it in the face of hostile surroundings is truly following in the footsteps of Jesus Christ who was put to death for living and proclaiming the Good News of salvation.

The man of faith is an affront to the modern atheist who reduces all reality to the eyes–ears–nose–throat level. Any statement or belief that cannot be verified by that criterion, in his view, must be dogmatically rejected as mythical or superstitious. The woman who believes in God and consequently rejects the here-and-now pleasure ethic of contemporary society is bound to be an object either of derision or pity from her "wiser" peers who "know better".

The convinced, practicing Christian is the person who walks by faith in the midst of every adversity. According to the letter to the Hebrews, faith is the "confident assurance concerning what we hope for, and conviction about things we do not see" (11:1). If you would like to read an inspiring passage from the Bible to mark the Lord's Day, I highly recommend this eleventh chapter of Hebrews. Here the inspired author recalls the heroes of faith in the Old Testament and reminds us of what they were able to accomplish for God because of their indomitable faith. He praises the faith of such people as Abel, Enoch, Noah, Abraham, Moses, Gideon, David and many others. These men believed in God, even though they did not always see where he was leading them and, Scripture says, because of their faith they were "approved by God" (Heb 11:2).

Faith in God gives a person a sense of direction in his life. The person of faith is confident that everything will work out for the best, for he knows that his eternal destiny and his earthly happiness are in the hands of a loving God. Thus the believer lives in a rational, orderly universe that is under the control of an all-wise, caring God. He is not the plaything of cruel fate or of implacable, impersonal forces, which was the idea that many of the ancient Greeks had with regard to man and his destiny.

It is true that there is a certain obscurity about faith, since what is believed is accepted on the authority of another—in this instance on the authority of God who can neither deceive nor be deceived. Hence, when a person assents to something as true on the basis of his faith, he does so not because he sees the intrinsic reason for the proposition in question (e.g., Trinity, Incarnation, grace, Resurrection), but because God himself has testified to this truth. The merit of faith is precisely in accepting something which we cannot prove by the power of human reason.

Faith, therefore, is rightly called a "submission" to God. It is obedience to God in the innermost depths of man—in his mind and in his will.

God spoke to Israel and elicited faith. Jesus spoke to the Jews and many believed in him. The Gospel was written down in order to strengthen the faith of Christians and to lead others to faith. St. John says that he wrote his Gospel "to help you believe that Jesus is the

24

Messiah, the Son of God, so that through this faith you may have life in his name" (Jn 20:31).

3

THE CENTER OF CHRISTIAN FAITH

The object toward which Catholic faith is directed is God himself. For we profess in the Creed "I believe in one God." The idea, however, that exists in the minds of different people in correspondence to the word "God" is not the same for all men and for all cultures. Many men have taken their idea of God from material things, thinking that he is the sun, the moon, the heavens, the earth, various animals, life forces, and so forth.

The Catholic Christian notion of God is based upon God's revelation of himself to man in the Old and the New Testaments. God graciously revealed himself to man in the course of salvation history, beginning from Adam and culminating in the Son of God, Jesus Christ. But even in the Old Testament, God revealed himself gradually to mankind through Israel, his chosen people. It is not until he personally appears in the flesh in Jesus Christ that we get a more profound understanding of the one God in three persons—Father, Son and Holy Spirit.

The one God that Christians believe in is the same God who guided the Israelites through their long, torturous history. During that time he was preparing them for the full revelation of himself in his only Son, Jesus Christ of Nazareth. Through the preaching, miracles, life, death and Resurrection of Jesus, a small group of believers was gathered together into the "Church" that professed its faith in the Triune God. By the divine assistance that "small flock" grew in numbers and extension so that it has by now touched practically every human culture and people on the face of the earth.

It is extremely important for Catholics to realize that the God they profess in the Creed is not just some abstract idea, like the God of the philosophers, who is logically deduced from the material world. Such a God is only an idea that may or may not refer to the eternal source of all being and reality. The more successful attempts along this line only reach God, as it were, from the outside. They tell man nothing about the inner nature of God, about God's plan for the world, about God's concern or unconcern for each and every person.

The God we Christians believe in has come incredibly close to us in Jesus of Nazareth. In and through Jesus he has told us about his own inner life. In Jesus he has and is reaching out to us in a gesture of love and he is asking (not forcing) us to respond in kind. That is the God we believe in and that is the God preached by the Church.

Even though, through Jesus, we know much about God, we must always remember that our knowledge is not comprehensive—it is in fact very defective. We know clearly what God wants us to do and what his plan is for the world, but we do not clearly see how God can be one and three at the same time: one nature and three divine Persons. At this point we approach the supreme mystery of the Christian faith. Jesus prays to his Father and sends the Holy Spirit upon his Church. We have all been baptized in the name of the Father and of the Son and of the Holy Spirit. *That* there are three Persons subsisting in one God we know from the New Testament, from the faith of the Fathers of the Church, from the liturgy and the preaching of the Church. *How* this can be we do not see. It is part of the merit of faith that we humbly accept this august, revealed truth on the Word of God.

4

THERE IS ONLY ONE GOD

One salient feature of religion is that there are many different religions and, correspondingly, many different ideas about the nature of God. With the advent of speedy travel to all corners of the globe and with satellite television news coverage daily from almost every country, we are today more than ever before aware of the great differences in religious belief.

In the Creed we profess belief in *one* God. What does the Church mean by this open confession of one God to the exclusion of all others? We are all seeking answers to the puzzling questions of our own personal existence. We are especially concerned about where we came from and where we are going. It is natural to man to ask these questions. He has been asking them, according to the record of history and literature, since the beginning of recorded time. It can also be shown from philosophy that man is by nature a questioning being. Unless impeded by others or by his own physical inability, man naturally asks questions about his own existence and the existence of the world in which he lives. And questions about existence necessarily lead to the question about God.

In the course of human history many different answers have been given to these questions. Fundamentally the answers are of three kinds: 1) God is immanent in the world and so identified with it; 2) God is transcendent and so completely separated from the world; 3) God is both immanent and transcendent but not in exactly the same way.

Because of the painful problem of evil, some (such as the Manicheans) have posited two gods caught in an eternal struggle—one, the source of good in the world, and the other, the source of evil. In this view, at different times one or the other is thought to subdue the other.

In the midst of many contrary ideas about God, the Bible says that there is only one God—the God of Abraham, Isaac and Jacob. Thus we read in Isaiah (44:6): "I am the first and I am the last; there is no God but me." The oneness of God is also taught in Job, chapter 38; Proverbs (8:23–30); Sirach, chapter 24; Wisdom (9:1–3).

In the New Testament St. John reports Jesus as saying: "This is eternal life, that they know thee the only true God, and Jesus Christ whom thou hast sent" (17:3). And St. Paul affirms that there is but "one Lord, one faith, one baptism, one God and Father of all, who is above all, and throughout all, and in all" (Eph 4:5–6).

28

Dangers to the true faith abound in every age. The chief danger at the present time in our thinking about God is to identify him so completely with the world, and especially with our fellow man, that he becomes in our minds totally immanent to the world. But the Catholic view of God is very precise and nuanced. There is only one God who is the Creator and sustainer of all that exists—and nothing exists without him.

The essential elements in the Catholic conception of God are his transcendence, infinity and personality. Through the revelation of Jesus we know that in the inner nature of God there are three Persons—Father, Son and Holy Spirit. God keeps everything in existence but he is not identified with any of his creatures. All creatures must be caused by some other being and that implies limitation and dependence. God is absolutely independent and so the source of everything that exists. Thus there can be only one God. The glory of the Christian is to know who the only true God is and to worship him in the Father, in the Son and in the Holy Spirit.

5

GOD OUR FATHER

In the Christian tradition, we are accustomed to call God our "Father". Jesus himself taught us to pray, "Our Father, who art in heaven, hallowed be thy name." And in the Creed, as soon as we profess our belief in one God, we immediately give him a personal name and designate him as the "Father".

To be a father, in the biological sense, means to communicate life and existence to another. For human beings, there is more to being a father than just generating a son or daughter. For a father not only generates—he also cares for his children by providing them with the material and spiritual things they need to grow up decently and enter into human society. In addition, the attentive father has a personal love for his children which elicits love from them in return. Since a father guides and directs his children until they can care for themselves, the notion of "father" includes the idea of authority over another, but normally in the sense of authority exercised in a spirit of love.

Of course we in America have some difficulties with these notions, since four out of ten marriages end up in divorce. This means that 40 per cent of our population grows up with a more or less distorted idea of what a father is. Also, due to our urban society, many fathers spend a great deal of time away from their families. There are, moreover, the constant attacks on the integrity of the family. The authority of the father seems to be diminishing while the authority of the peer group is increasing.

In spite of these and other cultural difficulties we might have with the notion of "father", it is fundamental to all human society and is at least understood by all—even by those who have never personally experienced the full depth of meaning of "father".

If we reflect a moment on who we are with our unlimited limitations, and who God is in his radiant infinity, it seems very bold to call God "Father". We are so weak. He is almighty. We are so sinful. He is holy. But Jesus teaches us in the Gospels to address God as "Father". When the disciples asked Jesus to teach them how to pray he told them to say, "Our Father. . . ." He told Mary Magdalene on that bright Easter morning in the garden to tell the Apostles, "I am ascending to my Father and your Father, to my God and your God" (Jn 20:17). For your Sunday Scriptural reading, I suggest that you read attentively the Sermon on the Mount, Matthew, chapters 5 to 7, and notice how often Jesus says "Father" when speaking of God. There he tells us to be perfect as the heavenly Father is perfect (Mt 5:48).

Because of our experience of fatherhood on the natural level, there is some justification in calling God "Father". The term was rarely used in the early books of the Old Testament, but became more common about two hundred years before Christ. It was Jesus, however, who really taught us to address God as "Father". Because Jesus is the only-begotten Son of God, having the same divine nature as the Father, there is a unique sense in which he calls God his Father. In his divine nature Jesus is the natural Son of the Father. By sending the Holy Spirit into our hearts—when we believe and accept baptism—

Jesus gives us a share in his own divine life and so we become *adopted* sons and daughters of the Father.

Today there is much talk about "human dignity". Our true dignity comes from the fact that God loves each one of us and has destined all of us to be his children. And since we are all sons of God in Christ, that means that we are all brothers. With Christ we can all say Abba—Father.

6

THE ALMIGHTY FATHER

In the Creed the Church attaches two attributes to the heavenly Father. She says that the Father is "almighty" and that he is the "maker of heaven and earth". Let us reflect a few moments on what it means to say that God the Father is "almighty".

When we say that the Father is almighty we mean first of all that his power is absolute or unlimited. This means that he can do everything that is "do-able". The only thing that God cannot do is something that would involve an intrinsic contradiction. For example, God cannot make a square circle because it is a nothing. Likewise, he cannot create a man who does not have a rational soul. For being able to think and love are essential to the very idea of being a man.

"Almighty" is the same thing as "omnipotent", which means to have all power, and it is the English translation of the Latin word used in the Creed, *omnipotens*. The omnipotence of God also presupposes his creative power. To create something means to produce it completely, without any preexisting material whatsoever. Whenever a man makes or "creates" something, he always has some material at hand to work with. One needs bricks, wood, nails, etc. in order to build a house. God's creative power is independent of all preexisting matter. He can produce things, as they say, "out of nothing"; "nothing" is not understood here as "something". When God makes something he produces its whole reality without the assistance of anyone or anything.

Some philosophers have said that God could produce things that are intrinsically contradictory. Such statements are false because they rest on the erroneous assumption that the intrinsic possibility of things is based not on the essence of God, but on his free will. Catholic thinkers have shown that before God can make anything it must first be possible as seen in his own essence. These reflections may seem abstract to some, but they are very important to our basic understanding of God. He is indeed all-powerful, as we profess in the Creed, but he is not at all capricious. Everything that God does he does for our greater spiritual good and also for our temporal welfare, so long as the latter is subordinate to the former.

Thinking about the almighty power of God should lead us to thoughts of deep humility, especially when we consider how weak we are. All the hydrogen bombs in the world are as a spark when compared with God's power. And a certain ambiguity always seems to surround human power—it can be employed either to aid us or to destroy us. Such is not the case with the almighty power of God. Our God is a loving God who makes his sun shine on the just and the unjust. In the physical universe he uses his power for our benefit. But his power also extends to the realms of the spirit. Here we find the amazing world of the angels, the realities of heaven, hell and purgatory, and the life of divine grace that is poured out upon us through the merits of Jesus Christ our Lord.

In the area of our own personal experience we have all come in contact with the power of God, whether it be a flaming sunset, a roaring ocean or the flutter of a yellow butterfly. But God's power is so vast that these are mere shadow reflections of the real thing. Since he loves us we glorify him and, with the psalmist, praise him for his almighty power.

7

MAKER OF HEAVEN AND EARTH

At the conclusion of the first part of the Creed we profess our belief that God the Father is the "maker of heaven and earth, of all that is seen and unseen". These words should draw our attention to the very beginning of the Bible, the book of Genesis, where we read that "in the beginning God created the heavens and the earth."

We have already discussed some of the characteristics of the divine creative power. In those first chapters of Genesis the "work" of God in fashioning the whole universe, including the earth, Adam and Eve, the animals, etc., is implicitly compared to the work of a potter who, with his turning equipment, makes various kinds of pots, jars and bowls. Thus, we read in Genesis (2:7) that "the Lord God fashioned man of dust from the soil."

The contemporaries of the ancient Hebrews had many views about the beginning of the world that are strange to us. Most of them tended to identify their gods with the world and with the various forces in the world that they could not control, such as the sun, the sky, the ocean, the life-force. Through his illuminating grace and his prophetic spokesmen God revealed to the chosen people of the Old Testament that he is completely transcendent, that is, above and independent of the material universe. He also revealed that he is immanent in it, in the sense that he gives life and being to all things but at the same time is not identified with them.

"Heaven" in the Creed also has the double meaning of the heavenly bodies such as the planets and the stars, and the spiritual dwelling place of the angels and saints. There also are to be found the resurrected Lord in his glorious humanity and the Blessed Virgin Mary who was assumed body and soul into heaven.

After saying that God made heaven and earth, the Church then repeats the same idea and at the same time becomes more precise by saying that he is the maker "of all that is seen and unseen". So not only is God the Creator of the visible universe, he is also the unique source of all invisible things, whatever they may be. From Scripture, human philosophy and science we know that there are many existing forces and beings that we cannot see. The unseen realities include both physical particles and forces, and the spiritual realms of angels and devils. What the Church is really doing in this profession is saying that all things whatsoever owe their origin and continued existence to God the Father.

Some philosophies and religions have maintained that parts of the universe did not proceed from God. The Manicheans even went so far as to say that there are two gods—a god of good and a god of evil. Biblical faith and the faith of the Church reject such dualism. The statement is all-inclusive. God the Father is the maker of all things—lofty, base, subtle and dense. Thus all things are open to his eyes and in his loving providence, according to the divine plan, he guides all things to their appointed goals.

8

JESUS IS LORD

I would like to call your attention to the fact that all of the prayers of the Church are directed to God the Father "through Jesus Christ, our Lord". Not only in the liturgy, but also in our religious conversation, we are accustomed to call Jesus "Lord".

After proclaiming our belief in one God in the first part of the Creed, we move on to profess our belief in Jesus Christ, the second Person of the Blessed Trinity. Since most of revelation comes through Jesus Christ, since he is one of us by reason of his being born into this world of the Blessed Virgin Mary in a certain place and at a certain time, and since we know more about him than we do about the other two divine Persons, we confess our belief in him in much more detail than we do in the case of the Father and the Holy Spirit.

"We believe in one Lord, Jesus Christ." The first affirmation we make about Jesus is that he is the Lord. The full meaning of the title includes the notions of authority, dominion, kingship and divinity.

In the Old Testament the title "Lord" or "*Kyrios*" was applied to Yahweh to signify his dominion over all things, including the gods of the pagans. In this sense he was also called the "Lord of lords". Toward the end of the Old Testament period the title "Lord" tended to replace the older "Yahweh", which was not even pronounced by pious Jews because of the sacredness of the name. Thus "Lord" came gradually to be used as the name of God himself.

In the Gospels, Jesus is rarely called "Lord", with the exception of a few times in Luke and John. The Apostles and first disciples did not come to the full realization that Jesus was God until after his Resurrection and after they had received the Holy Spirit at Pentecost. Once they had reached that realization they did not hesitate to attribute to him the divine title of "Lord" as used in the Old Testament.

When Jesus appeared to Thomas and showed him the wounds in his hands, feet and side, Thomas exclaimed "My Lord and my God!" (Jn 20:28). The profession "Jesus is Lord" was very common among the early Christians. St. Paul is constantly referring to Jesus as the "Lord", or he addresses his converts "in the Lord". In 1 Corinthians (12:3) he says, "No one can say 'Jesus is Lord' unless he is under the influence of the Holy Spirit." Paul claims that he is not preaching himself but "Christ Jesus as the Lord" (2 Cor 4:5). The Acts of the Apostles speaks a number of times about the first Christians being "baptized in the Lord".

As we shall see at a future date, the divinity of Jesus is asserted a number of times in the Creed. We first affirm our belief that he is God by attributing the divine title of "Lord" to him. Since he has dominion over all men and also over all creation, he has no superior and no equal. Therefore we say that we believe in "*one* Lord". Let us pray with St. Paul: "God raised him high and gave him the name which is above all other names so that all beings in the heavens, on earth and in the underworld should bend the knee at the name of Jesus and that every tongue should acclaim Jesus Christ as Lord, to the glory of God the Father" (Phil 2:9–11).

9

THE HOLY NAME OF JESUS

When the angel of the Lord appeared to St. Joseph in a dream he told him not to be afraid to take Mary as his wife and to name her child, "Jesus, because he is the one who is to save his people from their sins" (Mt 1:21). The name "Jesus" was a common one among the Israelites at the time our Savior was born and it means literally "Yahweh saves."

Among the ancient peoples a name did not just designate an individual person. It was not just a label used to distinguish one person from another. Rather, in one way or another it expressed the person's place in the universe by relating him to other beings. It could also express a man's activity or destiny. It is in this sense that our Lord was given the name "Jesus" because he is the Savior of the world, the Redeemer of the human race from sin, guilt and death. So the personal name of Jesus indicates his function in God's plan for mankind. Also, it gives a hint of the divine reality of Jesus as God himself, but in itself the name "Jesus" does not say that expressly. Other titles of Jesus, such as Lord, Son of Man, Son of God, Word, are needed to give a more complete communication of the divinity in Jesus that remains hidden behind the veil of the flesh visible to human eyes and accessible to human touch.

By the introduction of the holy name of "Jesus" in the Creed, we move into the realm of recorded history, of time and place. For, we profess that Jesus was born of the Virgin Mary, that he was crucified under Pontius Pilate (a Roman official about the year 30 A.D.), suffered, died and was buried. Thus, our Savior has a place in human history. He is not some distant god who appeared in the guise of a man for a short time and then disappeared. The pagan religions of the time tell stories of such "savior gods". This Jesus is truly one of us. He was born of Mary, belonged to the house of David, and lived in the town of Nazareth—a place that one can now travel to and walk around in. I know, for I was there just a few years ago, and I was very much moved by the place.

The name of Jesus had supreme importance among the first Christians. This stands out especially in the Acts of the Apostles. Peter cured a lame man "in the name of Jesus Christ the Nazarene" (Acts 3:6). Later, when the rulers in Jerusalem asked Peter about this incident, he replied, "Of all the names given to men, this is the only one by which we can be saved" (Acts 4:12). By appealing to the name of Jesus, his disciples cast out devils and worked all kinds of miracles. Jesus thus appears as his name indicates him to be: he who saves, and, especially, obtains eternal salvation for those who believe in him (Acts 4:7–12; 5:31; 13:23).

God has given Jesus "the name which is above all other names" (Phil 2:9), a new name which is not distinct from that of God himself. Thus, we can call Jesus of Nazareth both Lord and God.

To be a Christian means to believe that God has raised up Jesus from the dead, to confess that Jesus is Lord and to call upon the name of the Lord. Since Jesus is very God and God is the source of all holiness, then the name of Jesus is most holy. That sacred name should always be pronounced with reverence and respect.

10

CHRIST—THE ANOINTED ONE

We bear the name of "Christians" and are followers of Our Lord Jesus Christ. Let us concentrate for a few moments on the name "Christ" which became, in the first years after the Resurrection of the Lord, his proper name. For, in the Creed we profess our belief "in one Lord, Jesus Christ".

The word "Christ" is the English transliteration of the Greek word *Christos* which means "the anointed one". This Greek word, in turn, is a translation of the Hebrew and Aramaic *Messiah* which also means "anointed". During Lent we frequently see advertisements for performances or records of Handel's *Messiah*. So "Christ" and "Messiah" mean the very same thing.

The practice and notion of "anointing" are found in the Old Testament books of Samuel and Kings. These books recount the beginnings, history and disappearance of the kings of Israel, beginning with Saul, David and Solomon, and ending with the destruction of Jerusalem in 587 B.C., and the enslavement of the Jewish people by the Babylonians.

King David and his descendants were all anointed in their office as head and leader of the Chosen People. Scripture refers to the king as the "anointed of Yahweh". He was, therefore, a sacred person who, in a way, represented the kingship of Yahweh over his people. The people also believed that God worked through the king to protect them and to achieve his special plan.

When the kingdom was destroyed, the faithful began to look into the future for the Messiah (Christ) who would deliver them and establish an everlasting kingdom. The theological basis for this hope is the promise of the prophet Nathan contained in 2 Samuel (7:13), and repeated in Psalm 89 (28–29). I suggest that you take down your Bible and read these two passages.

In the course of time the title "Christ" underwent many changes, but we know for sure that at the time of Jesus it was understood mainly in a political and not in a theological sense. The feeling of the Messiah's imminent arrival was very intense.

Jesus himself was reserved in his attitude to the title. He forbade the demoniacs to say he was the Messiah (Lk 4:41); he told the twelve Apostles not to say that he was the Christ (Mt 16:20). The reason was that he did not want the people to get the wrong, political idea about his messiahship. His efforts were directed to give the title a transcendent, heavenly meaning. Finally, during his passion, when asked directly by the Jewish authorities, he admits that he is the Messiah (Mk 14:60–62). That was one of the reasons why they put him to death.

After the Resurrection, the first believers used the title "Christ" to sum up all the other titles. Gradually, what was once just a title became practically a proper name. Thus St. Paul, in his writings, is constantly referring to the Lord as "Jesus Christ" (cf. 1 Cor 1:1–9). The title-name was so important that within a few years the followers of Jesus of Nazareth were designated by it. "It was at Antioch that the disciples were first called 'Christians' " (Acts 11:26).

THE ONLY SON OF GOD

After professing our belief in "one Lord, Jesus Christ", we go on in the next phrase of the Creed to proclaim that he is "the only Son of God". We are also "sons of God" by reason of Baptism and the reception of divine grace, but we are sons with a small "s". Jesus is the Son of God with a capital "S".

The Old Testament was familiar with the idea of a son of God. At various times angels were referred to as "sons of God". The title is applied to the people Israel as a whole (Ex 4:22; Is 1:2; Hos 11:1). The title can also designate a devout person (Ps 73:15) and the Davidic king (2 Sam 7:14). In the Old Testament the idea behind the title is that a "son of God" has a special relationship to Yahweh that involves his protection and care.

In the New Testament the title "Son of God" is applied to Jesus in a very special way. The four Evangelists and St. Paul, writing many years after the Resurrection, knew and believed that Jesus was God and that he was therefore intimately related to God the Father and to God the Holy Spirit.

In his lifetime Jesus had often spoken of God as his father and he had prayed to God as his Father. Therefore Jesus was the Son in some very special senses. The Gospel according to St. Mark opens by saying: "The beginning of the Good News about Jesus Christ, the Son of God" (Mk 1:1). Both at Jesus' Baptism and at his Transfiguration a voice from heaven was heard saying,

"This is my Son, the Beloved; he enjoys my favor. Listen to him" (Mt 17:5; 3:17).

Perhaps the most dramatic confession of faith in the divine sonship of Jesus is that of Peter who, in reply to Jesus' question about who he is, said, "You are the Christ, the son of the living God" (Mt 16:16). All in all, the title "Son of God" is frequently applied to Jesus in the New Testament. We find it thirty-one times in the synoptic Gospels (Matthew, Mark, Luke), forty-two times in the Epistles and twenty-three times in the Gospel of St. John.

Just as "to be a father" means to have generated someone, so also "to be a son" means that one has been generated by someone. In our Catholic faith we profess our belief that the relationship between Jesus and God the Father is a relationship of Son to Father. We are dealing here with two distinct Persons but only one God. Both the Father and the Son share in the same divine nature. The Son resembles the Father in everything, except in the aspect of being a Father. In the coming essays we will go into more detail about the special relationship between Jesus and his Father and we will try to explain how it has been understood by the Church and by her greatest doctors of theology such as St. Athanasius and St. Thomas Aquinas. For, the next four phrases of the Creed explain in more detail what is meant by the title "Son of God".

For now let it suffice to say that Jesus is the "only" Son of God. By the word "only" the Church intends to say that Jesus is singular in that he is the perfect image of the Father. The Holy Spirit is also divine but he does not proceed from the Father in the same way that Jesus the

Son does. We are sons of God by adoption (faith and sanctifying grace). Only Jesus is the Son of God by nature. We profess this truth in the Creed. We should also try to make it a reality in our own lives.

12

FATHER AND SON

The Creed that we pray at Mass every Sunday devotes more space to explaining the unique relationship of Jesus, the Son, to the Father, than it does to any other single item. After proclaiming that Jesus is "the only Son of God", the Church goes on to say that he is "eternally begotten of the Father". We will now focus on this difficult expression.

When speaking of Father, Son and Holy Spirit we must always be very careful not to think and speak as if we are talking about three different gods. There is only one God, but in God there are three distinct *Persons*. The Creed explains in very succinct terms how the three Persons are related to each other. We would not even know that there are three Persons in one God if it were not for the revelation given to us by Jesus Christ, preserved and proclaimed by the infallible Roman Catholic Church.

By using the words "Father" and "Son" to designate

45

the first and second Persons of the Trinity, we are using an analogy from human relationships. A father *generates* his son and the son *is generated* by his father. As a result of the sexual activity known as "generation" a special relationship is established between the father who generates and the son who is generated.

Sex, of course, is dependent on having a body and being a material substance. God, as we know, is wholly spiritual and independent of all material things. So there is no sexual activity in God. But since we must think about God in terms that are intelligible to us, in order to understand how one Person proceeds from another, we use the terminology of father, son and generation. There is sufficient justification for this in Scripture since Jesus calls God his Father and refers to himself as the Son.

In a sense, a son is a reflection or image of his father. He has the same nature and frequently even looks like his father. In the inner divine life there is something similar to this. Jesus is the "image" of the Father (Col 1:15). He is also the Word of God (Jn 1:1). A word or thought is a reflection of the reality it refers to. Since God is Spirit, he is a thinking and loving being. God is also absolutely one and simple, having no multiplicity of being in him whatsoever. This means that God's thought is identified with himself and with his existence.

What the Church teaches in this matter, leaning almost completely on Scripture, is that the Son proceeds from the Father by a process we can call "generation" because the Son is the image of his Father. There is no sex involved, but since the Son (Jesus) is the perfect image of the Father and proceeds from the thought of the Father, there is some similarity between that and our experience of the relation between father and son. Hence, we proclaim that our Lord Jesus Christ is "eternally begotten of the Father". Please note that the Father begets only the Son, not the Holy Spirit.

Then there is that word "eternally". Eternity is opposed to time and it excludes all change and succession. Persons and things in time are subject to constant change. The Church says that Jesus is "eternally" begotten of the Father. The expression means that before the beginning of time the Son existed and always was the Son. There never was an age, so to speak, when the Son was not the Son.

This is difficult material but it is also important for our Christian faith. If it were not it would not be in the Creed. The essential points here are: 1) Jesus is the only Son of God, born of the Father; 2) from all eternity the Father has been Father and the Son has been Son. Thus the Son did not begin to exist with the conception of Jesus.

13

THE SON IS EQUAL TO THE FATHER

Since many heretics (particularly the Arians) in the early Church denied the divinity of Jesus Christ, the Church in her Creed or "rule of Catholic faith" pays special attention to the procession of the Son from the Father.

The Son or Word (cf. Jn 1) proceeds from the Father

by intellectual generation. This means that the thought or Word of the Father is a perfect image of himself. This Word, however, is not separate or distinct from the Father, since his thinking is identical with his existence.

Some early Christians thought that the Son of God was a creature or instrument of the Father, but not literally God. In order to reject that error the Church professes in her Creed that Jesus Christ, the eternally begotten Son of the Father, is *God from God*. Thus the Son is perfectly equal to God the Father in essence and being. There is no subordination in being of the Son to the Father. Just as the Father is eternal, so also is the Son. Just as the Father is all-powerful, so also is the Son, and so forth. Jesus Christ, therefore, is not the first creature produced by God the Father. He is rather his eternally only-begotten Son.

Jesus is also the *perfect* image of his Father, having in himself no defect or imperfection. In our experience as artists or builders we always find defects and a lack of correspondence between what we would like to make and what we actually produce. Thus, the painter is frequently dissatisfied with his painting because it does not measure up to the idea (e.g. of the Virgin Mary) that he had in his mind. In order to make it clear that there is no imperfection of this kind in the correspondence between the Son and the Father, the Church proclaims also that Jesus Christ is *light from light*. Because of the role of the sun in human existence and because of the purity and power of the light of the sun, the Church uses the example of light to exclude all notion of imperfection in the relationship between the Father and the Son.

What proceeds from another can also fail to equal the latter's reality because of some deficiency in truth; that is, it does not truly receive the same nature as the original but only imitates it in some way. Thus a picture of Pope John Paul on television is not the same thing as the Pope himself. It is only a likeness of him. To exclude all such deficiency from the divine generation of the Son, the Church adds to the rule of Catholic faith: *true God from true God*.

Since God's intellectual activity is identified with himself, it follows that he naturally understands himself. The object of his thought is not something outside of himself—something distinct from himself; rather, it is his own essence. Therefore, his Word or thought proceeds from himself naturally, as a father naturally generates a son. What we are saying here is that the Son is not produced artificially, as happens in the case where a man builds a boat or an artist paints a picture. Thus, in order to exclude the error of thinking that the Word of God proceeds from God not by way of nature, but by the power of the divine will or in any other way, the Church adds: *begotten, not made*.

Accordingly, the above four phrases in the Creed refer to the same reality in different ways, namely, that the Son is equal to the Father and therefore is God in the full sense of the word.

14

ONE IN BEING WITH THE FATHER

In the older translations of the Nicene Creed we used to profess of Jesus that he is "consubstantial with the Father". Since most Catholics are not acquainted with Greek philosophy and did not really know what the word "consubstantial" meant, the decision was made to translate the Latin *consubstantialis* (Greek: *homoousios*) by the English expression "one in Being" with the Father. The hope was that this expression would more clearly convey to all the faithful the orthodox belief of the Church concerning the relationship of Jesus to his Father.

In the third and fourth centuries one of the principal theological concerns was to define the exact relationship of Jesus the Son to the Father. The Arians said that the Son or Word was the first creature that God created—the noblest of all, but still a creature. This idea was not in accord with traditional Christian belief. It conflicted also with Scripture, for Jesus had said, "I and the Father are one" (Jn 10:30; 14:9–10). So it was a question of whether or not Jesus was fully divine. Is Jesus God in the same sense in which the Father is God?

There was much discussion about the question. Some of the early Fathers said that Jesus was "of one substance" with the Father. Some of the Greek Fathers, notably St. Athanasius, said that he is "consubstantial" (*homoousios*) with the Father. This was one of the questions that led to the calling of the first ecumenical council at the city of

Nicea, near Constantinople, in the year 325 A.D. The bishops at that council rejected the Arian contention that the Word of God (Jesus) is the first creature of the Father. They proclaimed instead that Catholic belief holds that the Son is fully equal to the Father. They said that he is "God from God, Light from Light, true God from true God, begotten, not made." Each of these expressions has its own particular meaning which we explained previously. The council then summarized all of these statements in the key expression, that was to become the test of orthodoxy, by adding that Jesus is "one in Being (consubstantial) with the Father".

We are dealing here with the Christian doctrine of the Trinity. In this matter it is always important to remember that there is only one God who is tri-personal —Father, Son and Holy Spirit. By saying that Jesus is "one in Being with the Father", the Church is asserting that Jesus is fully God, just as the Father is. Both share in the one divine nature or substance. Jesus proceeds from the Father but he retains the same being as the Father. Jesus is not a separate being from the Father, as is the case among creatures when a man and a woman generate a son. The son has the same *specific* nature as his parents, but he is a separate, independent being. Not so in the divine inner life. The Son is and exists by the same identical being as the Father does. This key idea was proclaimed by the first Council of Nicea and is now found in the Nicene Creed which has been prayed by the Church since that time. Some of the bishops at the Council of Nicea had difficulty with the expression "consubstantial" (*homoousios*) because it does not occur in the New Testament. The problem was resolved when they finally agreed that, even though the word itself is Greek in origin, the idea expressed by it is implied in the words of Jesus in the Gospels (see Jn 14:9–10).

The significance of the expression is that Jesus, who is one of us, is also God himself. This means that God is no longer removed from man. He has come near to us in Jesus of Nazareth. Now we know for sure that God loves us and is approachable.

15

THROUGH HIM ALL THINGS WERE MADE

Have you ever wondered why the Church in her Nicene Creed says that the Father is the "maker of heaven and earth", and then a few lines later says of the Lord Jesus that "through him all things were made"?

A basic principle of Catholic understanding of the creative activity of God is that all things outside of God himself, that is, all things visible and invisible, are produced by the divine essence or substance and so are to be attributed equally to the three divine Persons. Thus the notion of creation can be said of all three Persons. But when the Nicene Creed proclaims that "through him all things were made", it is referring to the doctrine of the Son as God's "Word" and so is speaking about the *inner* divine life. Let me explain what I mean by this.

We know from the Prologue of St. John's Gospel in chapter 1 that Jesus of Nazareth is the *Word* of God. Of this Word St. John says that He is: 1) eternal, 2) personal, 3) divine, 4) creative. In fact, the words of the Creed we are now considering come right from John (1:3): "He (the Word) was in the beginning with God; *all things were made through him*, and without him was not anything made that was made."

The key word to notice here is the preposition "through". Since God is Spirit, his inner life reflects what we refer to as "knowing" and "willing". For the essence of any spirit is to know and to will. Any time we utter a word to another we must first have some idea in our minds. And it is *through our ideas* that we both speak and make things. The carpenter must have an idea of the house he is going to build before he goes to work. It is *through* that idea, or *by means of* it that he is able to build the house. In a similar way, the Word of God is God's idea of himself. And the Word became flesh in Jesus of Nazareth.

The Word is consubstantial to the Father and therefore is equal to him in everything. Since God is Spirit, there is thinking in God. Thus, the Father is God as thinking and the Son is the same God as thought. The thought of God is called his "Word" and is identified with the essence of God.

Since the "Word" is God's thought, it is through that Word that God knows himself perfectly and all other things. Thus, if God freely wills to create or to produce something outside of himself he will have to produce those things "through" his own Word or idea. For, since God is the infinite source or cause of all reality, he must know all things that could possibly exist either in this world or in any other thinkable world. However, it should be carefully noted that the knowledge of God is not like our knowledge. Our knowledge is produced in our minds by our contact with things that exist prior to us and independently of us. With God the situation is just the reverse. By knowing himself he knows all things. Since God knows things in his own essence and has willed that they should exist outside of himself, they came into being. We must be careful not to think that God's knowledge is determined by creatures; for, if it were, that would mean that God was dependent on creatures for his knowledge of them. If that were so, God would not be God.

Where do such reflections lead us? They lead us to the conclusion that both the Father and the Son (the Word of God) are involved in creation. God the Father creates all things *through* the Word (Jn 1) who is his Son. The Jesus of the Gospels is the only Son of God. He is lovable and compassionate. But we should not forget that he is also our Creator—our first beginning and last end.

16

WHY DID GOD BECOME MAN?

One of the most common titles given to Jesus is that he is the "Savior". In fact, the notion of "Savior" is included in the very name of "Jesus" (see Mt 1:21). The Nicene Creed does not use the exact word "Savior" in speaking of Jesus, but it does state the reason why the Word of God became incarnate in Jesus of Nazareth: "For us men and for our salvation he came down from heaven."

So the purpose of the Incarnation was to effect the salvation of all mankind. St. Paul says in 1 Timothy (1:15) that "Christ Jesus came into this world to save sinners." In the Gospel of John we read: "For God so loved the world that he gave his only Son, that whoever believes in him should not perish but have eternal life. For God sent the Son into the world . . . that the world might be saved through him" (3:16–17). In the biblical use, "salvation" is related to redemption and liberation. In the book of Exodus, we read how God called his people out of Egypt, how he saved them from slavery under the Pharoah.

When the Bible and the Creed speak of "salvation" they are talking about the liberation of mankind from the power of sin, death and the devil. We know from revelation, especially from Genesis and the infallible teaching of the Church, that in the beginning God created man in a state of innocence and friendship with himself. As a result of man's rejection of God's love, he lost his original innocence, came under the power of sin and the devil, and was subject to death. Having lost God's grace, which was a pure gift to begin with and thus something to which he had no just claim, man became an outcast, unable to achieve the noble destiny to which God had ordained him.

Since man could not save himself from sin, could not by his own efforts regain the grace of God, God in his own infinite wisdom resolved to become man. Thus Jesus, the God-man, was able to make satisfaction to God's justice, for all of his actions had infinite worth. Very succinctly, therefore, the Creed proclaims that the reason for the Word becoming flesh was to accomplish the salvation of men. And when the Creed says "men" it means "all men" without any distinction as to race, color or creed. God's salvation is not restricted to the chosen people. In the writings of St. Paul we learn that faith in Christ was first offered to the Jews and then to the gentiles. Some Jews accepted it and some rejected it, just as some gentiles believed and some did not.

When the Church says that "he came down from heaven", she is referring to the pre-existence of the divine Word that became man in Jesus of Nazareth. Thus the Person who is Jesus existed from all eternity in the unity of Father, Son and Holy Spirit. The meaning is that he did not commence his existence with his conception in the womb of the Virgin Mary. He began to be in his human nature only.

In the faith-affirmation we are considering, there is also the idea of sacrifice and offering. This is said in a particular way by the preposition "for". Please note that in the consecration at Mass the Church directs the priest to say: "This is my body which will be given up *for you*," and "It [my blood] will be shed *for you and for all men* so

that sins may be forgiven." Thus our friendship with
God and our possibility of attaining eternal happiness in
the presence of God were attained for us by another. His
name is Jesus Christ.

17

THE ENFLESHMENT OF GOD

God became man in Jesus Christ for the eternal salvation
of all men. How did this take place? What does it mean?
In the Nicene Creed we proclaim: "By the power of the
Holy Spirit he was born of the Virgin Mary, and became
man."

In recent years there has been some questioning of the
New English translation of the Mass. Right here we run
into one of the problems because the original Greek
(*sarkotheis*) and Latin (*incarnatus*) do not say "he was
born" but "he took flesh" of the Virgin Mary. So the
English translation we use at Mass on Sunday is not
precise. You may recall the words of the Apostles' Creed
which are more exact in this matter, "He was conceived
by the Holy Spirit, born of the Virgin Mary."

This article of the Creed touches the heart and soul of
the mystery of Christ. Here are some of the truths it
contains.

1) The Son of God, the eternal Word, took flesh or
was conceived in the womb of the Blessed Virgin Mary.

By these words the ancient Fathers who composed the Creed rejected the errors of those who taught that Jesus only *appeared* to be a man, but did not actually assume a real human nature (they are called Docetists).

2) Jesus Christ was conceived without the agency of a human father or male sperm. For the Creed says that he was enfleshed "of the *Virgin* Mary". This is intended to reject the error of Valentinus, a second century heretic, who said that Jesus had a celestial body but not an earthly, material body. He is noted for having said that this body passed through the Virgin without receiving anything from her, just as water passes through a canal. The meaning of the Creed is that Mary supplied to Jesus everything that an ordinary human mother supplies to her child in the area of nutrition and gestation.

3) Jesus was conceived by the power of the Holy Spirit. There was no sexual intercourse involved in the conception of Jesus (see Lk 1:35). It was accomplished by the divine power properly disposing matter within the womb of the Virgin so that an ovum supplied by her was fertilized. We should not conclude from this that the Holy Spirit is the "father" of Jesus in the flesh. In his human nature Jesus did not have a father. To be a father means to generate in one's own likeness. The Holy Spirit, being God, does not generate Jesus' human nature in his own likeness, for he is infinitely above human nature. All activity of God outside the Trinity is common to all three Persons, but some actions are attributed to one Person rather than to another because of a special relationship to that Person. The Holy Spirit is the love of the Father and the Son, who love each other and us in him. Since God decreed that his Son should become incarnate because "of the great love with which he loved

us" (Eph 2:4), the formation of Christ's flesh is fittingly ascribed to the Holy Spirit.

4) The words "and he became man" were added to exclude the error that the Son of God "dwelt" in Jesus in some way, but did not actually become man.

The article of the Creed on the Incarnation is based on the explicit words of Scripture. St. John says, "And the Word became flesh and dwelt among us" (1:14). St. Paul writes to the Galatians, "When the time had fully come, God sent forth his son, born of a woman" (4:4).

In the above paragraphs I have tried to state as concisely as possible the truths contained in this article of the Creed. One could spend a lifetime profitably meditating on the meaning of the Enfleshment of God and never exhaust it. In the following section I will go into the purpose and meaning of the Incarnation and try to shed some light on what is involved for us personally and for all mankind when we profess that *God became man* in Jesus Christ.

18

AN ABSOLUTE MYSTERY

The Incarnation (God became man in Jesus Christ) is the central mystery of Christianity. Involved are both the meaning of man himself and the revealed reality of the Holy Trinity, for when we say that "God became man", we mean that the Word of God, the second Person of the Blessed Trinity, united to himself a human nature. So God became in Jesus what we are. It is the defined, official teaching of the Church that the Incarnation, as a term of the divine action, is the mysterious union of the divine nature and the human nature in the Person of the Word. This is also called the "Hypostatic Union", since the union of the divine nature and the human nature takes place in the Person of the Word. *Hypostatic* is the Greek word for "personal".

We are concerned here with an *absolute mystery* of the Catholic faith. Catholic theology distinguishes between relative and absolute mysteries of faith. A mystery is something "hidden" in the sense that we cannot understand it. A "relative" mystery is one that we human beings, in our present state, cannot understand but will be able to understand in our glorified state in heaven when we enjoy the face-to-face vision of God. An example of a relative mystery would be Jesus' raising Lazarus from the dead (Jn 11).

An "absolute" mystery of faith is something the reality of which cannot be known before its revelation and the inner possibility of which cannot positively be proved even after it has been revealed by God. There are three absolute mysteries of our Christian faith: the Holy Trinity, the Incarnation and divine grace.

So "Incarnation" means: God became man. This short sentence is filled with meaning for each one of us and for every man and woman on the face of the earth. For, by becoming man, God must have intended to tell us something important. God is not frivolous. He does not play games. If God became man in Jesus Christ, there must be a momentous reason for it.

We should ask ourselves: why? Why did God become a man almost two thousand years ago? The simple answer that Scripture gives is that God came into this world as a man to save us from sin. To save us both from original sin, for which Adam, not we, was responsible, and to save us also from our own personal sins for which we alone are responsible. St. Paul gives the reason for the Incarnation in 1 Timothy (1:15): "Christ Jesus came into this world to save sinners." The same idea is repeated often in the four Gospels and in the letters of St. Paul.

St. Thomas Aquinas argued that, even though the Incarnation was not absolutely necessary (since God could have redeemed man in other ways), there was a certain "necessity of convenience", a "fittingness" in the Incarnation of God. In addition to the idea of redemption from sin, Aquinas adds some other reasons for the Incarnation. He says that by the mysteries of his bodily life Jesus recalled men to a spiritual life; he showed the dignity of human nature; he demonstrated the immensity of God's love for us with a view to eliciting our return of love; he held up the ideal of a created intellect being united to uncreated Spirit; he offered man hope of obtaining the beatitude of eternal life.

These are some of the reasons given by Catholic theologians to help us understand why God became one of us. The further question of how God can "become" anything and still remain immutable in his own divine essence cannot be treated at this time. But we do know the fact, since John writes, "and the Word became flesh" (1:14).

The Incarnation says much about the goodness and love of God. It also says something about the dignity of man, for God chose to express himself, to make himself visible as a man. It is worth reflecting on and praying over the fact that the humanity of Jesus is eternally united to the Word of God in the glory of God the Father. That is a message of hope for you and me.

19

MORE REFLECTIONS
ON THE INCARNATION

It is a dogma of Catholic faith that God became man in Jesus. We profess our belief in this article of faith every time we pray the Creed. The more we reflect on this amazing truth, the more we should be astonished at the miracle of God's love for man.

Let us consider what the Incarnation means for us personally. First, it means that God became what we are. And what are we? We are weak, inconstant creatures, tied down by the limitations of time and space. We feel the tug of the earth and a powerful attraction for God. And who is God? God is the fullness of all being and perfection, eternal, all-powerful, all-good and loving. He is also our Creator, our first beginning and our last end.

Given that we are so needy and that God is the infinite source of everything that is, the incomprehensible element in the Incarnation is that God would deign to empty himself, to deprive himself as it were, in order to become man. St. Paul says of Jesus that "though he was in the form of God, he did not count equality with God a thing to be grasped, but emptied himself, taking the form of a servant, being born in the likeness of men" (Phil 2:6–7). So God became like us in all things except sin.

Various Christian thinkers in the past have strayed from the truth in their attempts to explain this sublime mystery of the Enfleshment of God, because they could not fundamentally accept the reality that *God became man*. Some said that Jesus was a holy man who was "adopted" by God and elevated to the level of the divine. Others said that Jesus, though God himself, only appeared to be man but was not actually made of flesh and blood as we are. Others said that the Word of God, who is the Person of Christ, is not himself God but only the first and most noble creature of God. There are more variations on the same theme. They all come down to denying that Jesus Christ is true God and true man, consubstantial with God in his divinity and consubstantial with us in his humanity.

If any of these christological theories were true, then it would follow that God did not really become man, that the Son of God did not unite to himself hypostatically our human nature, that the sacraments are useless and the Church is a fraud. If the above views were true, then those tremendous words "and the Word was made flesh and dwelt among us" in John 1:14 would be false. In short, the entire kerygma of the Church, that is, the preaching about the life, miracles, death and Resurrection of Jesus, would be a lie. Hence, the Church in the fourth and fifth centuries reacted very strongly to these ideas, completely rejected them and branded them for all time as "heretical".

On the positive side, the Incarnation means that by becoming man God has taken to himself the reality of the material world. In Jesus Christ we know that God loves us. His love for us is so great that he "emptied" himself, in the words of St. Paul, in order to become one of us. He did this not for himself, but "for us men and for our salvation".

The message of salvation in Jesus is almost too great and too good to be true. But we know it is true because of the life and death of Jesus, who was the first Witness, the first Martyr. The Apostles gave witness to this truth with their blood. The same can be said for countless thousands of saints and martyrs.

Because of the Incarnation Christianity is a religion of hope and not of despair. God came so very close to us in Jesus of Nazareth. In him God demonstrated his love for us and is now calling to us for our response of love.

20

JESUS SUFFERED FOR OUR SAKE

After affirming the divinity of Jesus Christ by stating that he is the Son of God and equal to the Father, the Nicene Creed turns, with a few quick, deft strokes, to his passion and death. It is remarkable that the Creed says nothing about the private and public life of Jesus. It passes over his miracles, his prophecies and his profound teachings about God and man.

The last day in Jesus' earthly existence is summ&d up in the words: "For our sake he was crucified under Pontius Pilate; he suffered, died and was buried."

In the previous sentence the Creed proclaimed: "For us men and for our salvation he came down from heaven." As if to drive this point home, the Creed prefaces its short account of the passion by reminding us that Jesus suffered, not for himself, but "for our sake". Sinless as he was, there was no need for him to be crucified in order to save himself. He did not need redemption. We are the sinful ones who are desperately dependent upon a savior.

By mentioning the Roman governor Pontius Pilate, the Creed clearly locates the passion and death of Jesus in human history. We are not dealing here with some philosophical theory that could happen anywhere any-time. Pilate was governor of Judea in Palestine about the year 30 A.D. That is a fact that can be established by profane history. Jesus, therefore, being a member of the Jewish race, was put to death under this Roman official in Palestine.

Crucifixion was the most severe form of capital pun-ishment in Roman law. It was considered so degrading that it could not be applied in the case of Roman citizens. It was reserved for slaves, robbers and brigands. Jesus had foretold what kind of death he would die when he said: "And I, if I be lifted up, will draw all things to myself" (Jn 12:32). Crucifixion, certainly, was a most severe form of suffering, followed by sure death.

To suffer means to endure some kind of harm. Since man is spirit in a material body, he can suffer both in his soul and in his body. Thus when Jesus suffered rejection, ridicule, betrayal of Judas, scourging, the crowning of thorns, he endured harm in both body and soul. He was able to do this because, in assuming our human nature, he took upon himself all those defects that are common to man, such as subjection to hunger, thirst, weariness and physical violence of all kinds. However, since Jesus enjoyed the immediate vision of God in his soul, he did not share in the defects of our soul, such as sin and ignorance.

"Suffering" is a bad word for most of us. We would rather not hear the word. We don't like to think about what it means. And we shun the reality in any way we can. Just think of the *billions* of white, red, green and blue pills that are sold each year in this country. Most of them were devised to help people avoid suffering. Yet the Creed says simply of Jesus: "He suffered."

The major difference between the suffering of Jesus and our suffering is that he freely willed and accepted it. By freely assuming our human nature, Jesus accepted everything that goes with it, sin alone excepted. We weak human beings are not able to control the forces of nature. Hence, we are subject to suffering of all kinds because we cannot control the world around us. Jesus' situation was different. With his divine knowledge he knew everything. With his divine power he was capable of warding off any threat. Note what he said in Gethsemane: "Do you think that I cannot appeal to my Father, and he will at once send me more than twelve legions of angels?" (Mt 26:53).

We should ask ourselves why Jesus suffered. The answer is: *for our sake*. Because of the first sin of Adam we were cut off from the life of grace, excluded from heaven and condemned to die. Jesus took it upon himself to make satisfaction for us and so to pour out the grace of God upon us. It was part of the mysterious plan of God, hidden from all eternity, that this should be accomplished by the suffering and death of the Christ, the "man of sorrows" (Is 53:3).

21

THE DEATH OF JESUS

In the Nicene Creed we profess that Jesus "died and was buried". These are the final affirmations in the Creed about the earthly life of the Savior of mankind.

All men are under the certain, sad sentence of death. Death, as we know from Romans 5 and 6, is the consequence of sin. "The wages of sin is death," writes St. Paul (Rom 6:23). When God first created man, he did not destine him for death (cf. Gen 2–3). The official doctrine of the Church on this truth was spelled out in detail by the Council of Trent.

Philosophically, death means the separation of the soul from the body. There is both a personal and an impersonal dimension to the meaning of death. On the impersonal plane, it means that biological and physical forces overpower man to such an extent that his soul can no longer animate the body. The signs of death are the cessation of biological functions and the beginning of corruption.

On the personal plane, death means that our spiritual growth and our exercise of human freedom in time come to a brutal halt. As adults, we determine ourselves according to our likes and dislikes, our aspirations and our fears. In death, we are determined by powers beyond our control and contrary to our will.

Man lives his whole life under the shadow of death. It is our constant companion, whether we explicitly advert to it at each moment or not. Man fears death and senses, somehow, that it should not be, that it is beneath his dignity to have to submit to physical dissolution.

The above is a very brief sketch of death. The point here is that Jesus Christ, the sinless One, submitted to the power of death which had no right to claim him. He died our death in order to save us from eternal death and open up to us the life of God. Thus St. Peter says: "Christ also died once for our sins, the just for the unjust, that he might offer us to God, being put to death indeed in the flesh, but enlivened in the spirit" (1 Pet 3:18).

The death of Jesus was a true death, not just an apparent one. This means that when "he cried out with a loud voice" (Mt 27:50) on the cross and gave up his spirit to God, his human soul, which is of the same nature as our souls, left his torn and bloody body.

In the Apostles' Creed, which we traditionally pray at the beginning of the Rosary, we add after the death and burial of Jesus that "He descended into hell." This expression is not included in the Nicene Creed, but it means that the soul of Jesus was truly separated from his body, that he was dead, and that his pure soul entered into the realm of the dead—called by the Jews *Sheol* or the "underworld". It does not mean that he was punished in hell in the usual Christian sense of the place and state of eternal torment. It was the obedient death of Jesus that threw open the gates of heaven. Thus, according to Catholic belief, in the period after his death and before his Resurrection, he set free all the saved who were detained in *Sheol* from the time of Adam to Calvary.

Christ died. After his death he was buried according to the Jewish custom. In this he also shared our lot, with the exception that his body was not to see corruption. This is in accordance with Psalm 16 (10): "You will not give your holy one to see corruption." According to St. Thomas, the reason for this is that although Christ's body was formed from earthly matter as ours is, its formation was not by any human power but by the power of the Holy Spirit. Hence he did not wish the body that had been formed by the Holy Spirit to undergo dissolution, since in this respect he was different from other men.

22

THE RESURRECTION OF JESUS

"On the third day he rose again." With these words the Creed moves from the earthly life of Our Lord to the glorious state in which he now lives. It is to be noted that Jesus' Resurrection from the dead is mentioned in all of the early creeds of the Church.

Jesus died on Friday afternoon about 3:00 P.M. and was immediately laid in the tomb before dark. According to the Jewish reckoning of time, a day is calculated from nightfall to nightfall. Since Jesus was buried Friday afternoon and rose from the dead on Easter Sunday, he was in the ground during some part of three different days. Hence, the Creed correctly says that he rose "on the third day", that is, the third day from his death and burial. St. Gregory the Great thought that the Resurrection took place at midnight between Saturday and Sunday, but St. Augustine and others have been of the opinion that it took place at dawn and so it is usually represented in Christian art.

Our English version of the Creed says that Jesus rose "again". Normally when we use the word "again" we mean "a second or third time". Obviously it cannot mean that in the Creed since Christ died once and rose once from the dead. Then why do we say "again"? The word can also mean "on the other hand", "in addition". So it can also have an adversative meaning—and that is the way it is used in the Creed. After saying that he died and was buried, the Creed says, "however", on the third day he rose. If you read the phrases over in succession you will understand the contrast.

We all know what the Resurrection of Jesus means and again we do not understand it. At present I am going to consider *Jesus'* Resurrection—later there will be something to say about our own personal resurrection, since that is also affirmed in the last sentence of the Creed.

"Resurrection" means the return of a dead man to life in its most literal sense. So the Creed simply says that Jesus, who died on the Cross on Friday and whose corpse was laid in the tomb, came back to life on Sunday. This is indeed a shocking statement. It signifies something that we have never experienced but must accept solely on faith because of the testimony of the Apostles, for the Apostles were the chief witnesses of the Resurrection (cf. Acts 2:32; 3:15; 5:32).

During his apostolic ministry, Jesus raised people from the dead. There was the twelve-year-old daughter of Jairus (Mk 5:21–42), the only son of the widow of Naim (Lk 7:11–17) and his own personal friend, Lazarus, the brother of Mary and Martha (Jn 11). But they were raised to continue their natural human life on earth. As such, they had to die a second time. Not so with Jesus. Jesus rose from the dead to a new and glorious form of life that will never end.

As we have already seen, Jesus died a cruel death on the Cross on Good Friday. His human soul departed from his body. According to the words of Scripture, during this time Christ's soul was in the "underworld" or *Sheol* and set free into heaven the souls of all the just who had died since the time of Adam. After about thirty-eight hours, the pure soul of Christ returned to be re-united with his body. Jesus returned to life. But what a life! His new life is very different from ours. We must always remember that when we are speaking of the Resurrection of Jesus we are talking about a divine mystery. In the Resurrection, the glorified humanity of Jesus has taken on qualities that we know little or nothing about.

Jesus is now living at the "right hand of the Father". He appeared to the frightened Apostles suddenly, "the doors being shut" (Jn 20:19, 26). Whole books can and have been written on the Resurrection of Jesus.

23

THE GLORIFIED BODY OF JESUS

After his Resurrection from the dead, Jesus manifested himself to his disciples in different ways and on different occasions. He appeared to Mary Magdalene and at first she thought he was the gardener (Jn 20:11–20). He appeared to the two disciples on the road to Emmaus. During their walk and conversation they did not recognize him, but when he broke bread for them they knew that it was the Lord (Lk 24:13–35).

There is something hauntingly mysterious about Jesus' appearances after his Resurrection. The Gospels give testimony that Jesus did indeed return to life on Easter Sunday, but to a life that was much different. It is the same Jesus, but now he appears suddenly inside the upper chamber, "the doors being shut" (Jn 20:19). We do not really know what the qualities of the resurrected body are, but from the Gospel accounts it does seem that Jesus' body possesses power over material things in a way that is beyond our experience and knowledge.

We know that two bodies cannot occupy the same space at the same time. Still, the glorified Jesus passes through walls like light through a window. He is able to converse and associate with disciples who knew him well, such as Mary Magdalene and the two men on the way to Emmaus, but he does not allow them to recognize him. This means that he can let them see him but they can recognize him only if he so wills. Again, this shows that Jesus has power over his body that vastly exceeds anything we are familiar with, except perhaps in the creative imagination of science fiction.

One conclusion that follows from the Gospel accounts of the appearances of Jesus is that matter has capabilities that modern man, whether scientist or not, knows nothing about.

In order to confirm the faith of his disciples in his Resurrection, Jesus had to convince them that it was really he. All four Gospels mention the Resurrection, and each gives some details regarding the appearances (cf. Mt 28; Mk 16; Lk 24; Jn 20–21). First of all, they recognized him in his physical appearance—his body was the same body, though transformed, that they had known during the preceding three years. Thomas doubted, so the Lord said to him: "Put your finger here and see my hands; and put out your hand and place it in my side; do not be faithless, but believing" (Jn 20:27). To all of the assembled disciples, he said: "See my hands and my feet, that it is I myself; handle me, and see; for a spirit has not flesh and bones as you see that I have" (Lk 24:39).

Jesus also showed that he was the same Person by his mannerisms—the way he spoke, his tone of voice, the way he ate and drank and broke bread. By these and other signs he proved to them that it was really he and that he was now enjoying a completely new and different kind of life.

It is difficult for man to believe in the resurrection of his body, and there are many today, including some Christians, who do not believe it. Death is all around us and there is a terrible finality about it. Jesus had foretold his Resurrection, but his followers had not grasped it. Thomas would not believe it even after the other ten Apostles had seen the risen Lord. He demanded special proofs. Because of this innate difficulty for man to believe in the Resurrection, Jesus went to great lengths to establish the reality of his Resurrection for his Apostles. He showed them some aspects of his glory, but not all of it. For if he had shown them the fullness of his glory, it would have been too overpowering for them and they would have been tempted to think that it was not the same Jesus they had walked with on the dusty paths of Judea and Galilee.

Thus, by his many appearances and his gentle ways, Jesus aroused and confirmed the faith of his Apostles in his Resurrection. They knew it was the *same Lord* now living a new, *glorified life*.

24

THE COSMIC EFFECTS
OF JESUS' RESURRECTION

Have we become so familiar with the Christian affirmation of Jesus' Resurrection from the dead that we are no
longer really aware of the cosmic implications of that
assertion? There is no doubt that the Resurrection was
the center of the apostolic preaching (see Acts 2; 3; 4; 10;
1 Cor 15). The Apostles were primarily *witnesses* to the
Resurrection.

Since Jesus is truly risen from the dead and living to
make intercession for us at the right hand of the Father,
this passing world of suffering and death is not the same
as it was prior to his Resurrection and glorification.
For, one of us—a member of our human race and a de-
scendant of Adam—has entered into the glory of God.
The God-Man Jesus Christ, fully human just as we are
and remaining a member of our race, has taken on a new
spiritual existence. In the words of St. Paul, he has
become "a life-giving spirit" (1 Cor 15:45). He is "the
first fruits of those that have fallen asleep" (1 Cor 15:20).
"He is the beginning, the first-born from the dead, that
in everything he might be pre-eminent" (Col 1:18).

According to our human experience, everything in
this world is passing away—and quickly. Cultures rise
and fall. Powerful states like Athens, Rome and Czarist
Russia come and go. Some merit a chapter perhaps in our
history books, while others receive only a page or a
footnote. But no matter what living conditions man

finds himself in, his plight in this world is always precarious. His life is short, filled with some joy, but mostly it is a story of suffering, misunderstandings, disappointments and sorrow. Men disagree on many things, but there is no serious disagreement about the universality and finality of death for all men and women.

We know from the revelation brought to us by Jesus Christ what the source of all man's problems is: it is *sin*. Sin is the cause of death and all of the human suffering that surrounds it (see Rom 5:12–21). The point of Jesus' death and Resurrection is that he has basically solved these two problems of sin and death. By his own death on the Cross he overcame sin, and by his glorious Resurrection from the dead he destroyed death in principle and restored man to life. That is what the mystery of Christ is all about.

Because of the Resurrection of Jesus, therefore, this old world is no longer what it seems to be, at least for the person who has faith in Jesus Christ. The world has taken on a new face. The Resurrection is the object of our faith and the basis of our hope. Jesus is "the first-born of all creation"; "He is before all things, and in him all things hold together"; God wishes "through him to reconcile all things, whether on earth or in heaven, making peace by the blood of his cross" (Col 1:15–20). Because of his obedience, "God has highly exalted him and bestowed on him the name which is above every name, that at the name of Jesus every knee should bend, in heaven and on earth and under the earth" (Phil 2:9–10).

Because of Jesus' Resurrection, death is not what it seems to be. It is not the end, but the beginning of a new type of life for the saved. While remaining human beings of flesh and blood, we shall all be transformed (1 Cor

76

15:51) into "spiritual bodies" (1 Cor 15:44). And God plans, in the fullness of time, "to unite all things in him (Christ), things in heaven and things on earth" (Eph 1:10).

Thus the Resurrection of Christ has already had a profound influence on the whole cosmos. Not all men are now aware of this change, but they shall be at the end of the world. At present it is only the believing Christian who knows this truth by faith. He also experiences it, though in a veiled way, through his experience of the grace of God and when he sincerely proclaims in the Nicene Creed: "On the third day he rose again in fulfillment of the Scriptures."

25

JESUS ASCENDED INTO HEAVEN

On top of the Mount of Olives in Jerusalem is situated the small, hexagonal "Church of the Ascension" which commemorates Jesus' final departure from his disciples and from this world (Acts 1:12). In the Nicene Creed, we profess our belief in Jesus' Ascension when we say: "He ascended into heaven and is seated at the right hand of the Father."

The Ascension is a mystery of faith, just like Jesus' Resurrection, with which it is closely associated. The event is mentioned briefly by the Evangelists Mark

(16:19) and Luke (24:50–53). A more detailed account is given by Luke in the Acts of the Apostles (1:1–12).

The Ascension of Jesus can be defined as the transfer of his risen, glorious body to heaven, that is, to the world of the divine. In the Old Testament, God is described in some texts as "descending" from heaven to accomplish something on earth; he then "ascends" or returns to the world of the divine. Jesus himself speaks of descending to this earth and ascending again to the Father once his work of redemption has been accomplished (cf. Jn 3:13, Eph 4:10).

Except for the mention of the forty days by Luke in Acts, Mark, Luke and John think of the Ascension as occurring on the day of the Resurrection. The idea is that the final glorification and exaltation of Jesus takes place at his Resurrection—they are two aspects of the same thing. Through his Resurrection-Ascension, he leaves the earth and the created universe to take his place at the right hand of the Father.

The image of sitting "at the right hand of the Father" is influenced by Psalm 110 (1): "The Lord said to my lord: 'Sit at my right hand, till I make your enemies your footstool.'" The image itself comes from the ancient world of kings and courts where the all-powerful king was surrounded by his ministers, with the most powerful and favored one sitting just to the right of the king. Hence, it means in this case that Jesus is one with the Father and shares in his sovereign power over the world and the cosmos.

If Jesus had not entered immediately into his final glory at the Resurrection, it would be difficult to explain where he was during the interim between the Resurrection and the Ascension. We are dealing here with a divine mystery and it is hard for us to grasp the full meaning.

There are enough indications in the Gospel accounts of the appearances of Jesus to support the belief that he was already in the glory of the Father when he appeared to his followers. But there was a period of instruction after the Resurrection during which Jesus gave his Apostles their final preparation before going out to bear witness to him to the ends of the earth. So it is commonly held that the Ascension means the final appearance of Jesus to his Apostles before his definitive departure for heaven. Thus the Ascension has a pedagogical character.

The number "forty" in Scripture means a full period of time, a rounded-out period; it does not necessarily mean literally forty calendar days. In this context, then, it means that Jesus appeared to his disciples regularly for a period and then left them permanently. From then on they had to live by faith and communicate with him through prayer and the sacraments.

Thus, this mystery has two aspects: 1) the heavenly glorification of Christ which coincided with his Resurrection, and 2) his final departure from his Apostles after a period of apparitions. The feast of the Ascension commemorates this second aspect.

The Ascension means that Jesus, triumphant over death, has begun a new life with God. He has gone to heaven to prepare a place for the elect. On the Last Day, he will return to lead them there so that they might take up their abode with him (Jn 14:2 ff.). For this reason, the Ascension is a source of great hope and consolation for Christians.

26

THE SECOND COMING

After professing the Resurrection and Ascension of Jesus at the right hand of the Father, the Nicene Creed next affirms: "He will come again in glory to judge the living and the dead, and his kingdom will have no end." Since there is much material here for fruitful reflective thought, we will take one truth at a time, beginning with the Christian belief that Jesus will come again.

Though not stressed much today, the idea of the Second Coming of Jesus occurs frequently in the New Testament. It is also called the "Day of the Lord" and the "Parousia", which means the "presence" or "arrival" of someone.

By the expression "the Second Coming", we are referring to the Christian belief in the words of Jesus that he will come again in glory to judge all men. The Parousia will signal the end of human history as we know it. When this will take place no one knows but the Father (Acts 1:11), nor is there any clear indication in Scripture of just how it will be accomplished.

In popular language we usually refer to these events as "the end of the world", which is itself not completely accurate, since the Day of the Lord does not mean that the universe as we know it will be *annihilated*, but only that it will be changed into something new and wonderful—something that surpasses the imagination of man.

The New Testament gives some intimations of the

signs that the Lord is about to come and judge the world. There is mention of wars, famines, earthquakes, upheavals in the planets and the stars. These "signs" are borrowed from the apocalyptic language of the Old Testament, especially as it is found in Daniel 7 and in the prophet Joel.

The Second or final Coming of Jesus in glory is contrasted with his first coming in humility as the Son of Mary and Joseph. So the Incarnation is spoken of as his first appearance to mankind. Through his death-Resurrection-Ascension, Jesus passed from this life to a new and glorious life in heaven. From there he sends out the Holy Spirit on his Church. Now he is present in our midst through faith, through the preaching of the Gospel and in the sacraments.

In many places, the New Testament mentions the Parousia of the Lord. "They will see the Son of man coming on the clouds of heaven" (Mt 24:30); "If it is my will that he (John) remain until I come, what is that to you?" (Jn 21:23); "This Jesus . . . will come in the same way as you saw him go into heaven" (Acts 1:11).

When Jesus comes again in glory, human history will be terminated. All will be transformed, both the living and the dead (see 1 Cor 15:51–56). Thus everything now is provisional. There was a current of thought among early Christians, reflected strongly in St. Paul's two letters to the Thessalonians, that the glorified Lord would come soon. This is to be understood as a *hope* and an expectation that the Lord would soon come and establish his definitive kingdom by destroying all of the powers of sin and evil. It was not a firm conviction or a certain judgment.

To the early Christians the Second Coming of Jesus,

which was understood as the consummation of God's work in redeeming the human race, was not something to be feared. Rather, it was hoped for, longed for. They fervently prayed, "Come, Lord" (1 Cor 16:22). In fact, the next-to-last sentence of the entire Bible reflects this longing, first by quoting Jesus himself, and then by adding a prayer: " 'Surely I am coming soon.' Amen. Come, Lord Jesus!" (Rev 22:20). As believing, hoping followers of Jesus Christ, this should also be our prayer.

27

THE GLORY OF THE LORD

The Nicene Creed says not only that Jesus "will come again" at the end of world history, but it also gives a biblical description of his coming by adding that he will come "in glory". The idea of "glory" and the "glory of God" occurs throughout the Bible, so we might do well to reflect on this datum of revelation for a few moments.

In the Hebrew Bible the word for "glory" (*kâbôd*) originally meant weightiness. If something was heavy and large it was important, like a mountain, and so it inspired respect. The basis of glory could be riches. Abraham was said to be "very glorious" because he possessed cattle, silver and gold (Gen 13:2).

The expression "the glory of the Lord" means God himself insofar as he is revealed in his majesty, his power and his holiness. He manifests himself in two ways: in his lofty deeds and by his appearances to Abraham, Moses and the prophets. God showed his glory especially in the miracle of the Red Sea (Ex 14:18) and also in the manna and the quail (Ex 16:7). The divine appearances are normally accompanied with disturbances of nature, such as thunder, lightning, fire, earthquakes, clouds. These phenomena manifest the glory of God; the cloud that surrounds the glory is there for the protection of man, for no man can see God and still live (Ex 33:20).

The glory of God, in the form of a cloud, filled the Tent of Meeting where Moses spoke with the Lord (Ex 33:9). It also filled "the house of the Lord" that Solomon built (1 Kings 8:10–11). As time went on the idea of God's glory developed in the prophets from clouds and fire to the notion of *illumination*. We find this in Ezekiel 1 and Isaiah 60.

After the Exile (537 B.C.), the Jews came more and more to realize that the power of the Lord extended over the whole world. Thus his glory is shown in his *dominion* over all nations and all creatures. The Psalms often call upon all creatures to praise the glory of the Lord (cf. Ps 57; 97; 145–50). But the one passage in the Old Testament to which the "coming in glory" of the Creed refers, more than to all others, is the description of the "son of man" in the prophet Daniel (7:13–14): "I saw one like a son of man coming on the clouds of heaven. . . . He received dominion, glory and kingship; nations and peoples of every language serve him." This passage is commonly interpreted as referring to Jesus Christ who will "come in glory to judge the living and the dead".

Glory in the sense of majesty, power, dominion, illumination, holiness belongs primarily to God. Men like Moses or the saints can share in the glory of God by doing his will and by growing in virtue.

Isaiah says that "all the earth is filled with his glory" (Is 6:3). The glory of God in this sense can mean: 1) the divine perfection, and 2) the praise that creatures give to God because of his glory. The sense of this text from Isaiah is that all creatures reflect the wisdom and perfection of God. And by their very existence, as a reflection of God's perfection, they give praise to their Creator. Man alone among all creatures on earth gives praise to the glory of God not only by his physical existence, but also by consciously acknowledging the goodness and the love of God.

The motto of St. Ignatius Loyola, founder of the Jesuit Order, was *Ad Maiorem Dei Gloriam*—"For the Greater Glory of God". The phrase came so spontaneously to his lips that it appears on almost every page he ever wrote. Ignatius was so captivated by the love and goodness of God that he would spare no effort to give recognition to God and to praise him by a life of virtue and sacrifice.

Christian painters surround their images of Christ and the saints with reds and yellows and white to indicate their glory. This is an attempt, through the impression of illumination, to indicate their glory. By faith, we know that Jesus Christ will come again in glory—the blazing light, clouds and fire are symbols of his definitive triumph over evil and death and his everlasting dominion.

28

JESUS WILL JUDGE
THE LIVING AND THE DEAD

We have already considered the glorification and the Second Coming of Jesus. If we ask ourselves what Jesus is going to do when he comes again, we can look to the New Testament and to the Creed for the answer: He is coming to judge the living and the dead.

The thought of judgment is not very congenial to us. The notion is most usually associated with criminal courts and wrongdoing of one sort or another. There is a problem involved in deciding who is right and who is wrong, or who is guilty and who is innocent. Because we are social beings and live together in community, there are bound to be conflicts of rights. In order to resolve such conflicts there is need for judgment and judges. Though necessary, the process is painful and we would like to avoid it if at all possible.

When it comes to our relationship with God we are especially apprehensive about the prospect of being judged by him. For "all things are naked and open to his eyes", as we read in Hebrews (4:13), and not one of us is sinless.

From our catechetical instruction we know that the Church teaches a twofold judgment of God: the particular judgment that each one experiences immediately after death, and the general judgment that will take place at the end of the world or the Second Coming of Christ when the historical process will be brought to a close.

The judgment of God in this sense is the final act whereby he settles forever the destiny of the free creature —either to eternal punishment in hell or to eternal reward in heaven. The basis of God's judgment is faith and good works or charity. Those who believe and live their faith accordingly will be saved; those who believe but do not love God and neighbor will be condemned; those who refuse to believe that Jesus is the Christ and those who, not having heard about Christ, refuse the grace of God that is given to them (1 Tim 2:4), will also be lost.

When the Creed says that Jesus will judge "the living and the dead", it means that he will judge *all* men—past, present and future. No person will escape his judgment. Since all men are subject to sin (Rom 5), they are all likewise subject to death (Rom 6:23). Even Christ and Mary had to die. Some have interpreted "the living" in the Creed to mean those in the state of grace, and "the dead" to mean those in sin. However, "the living" can also mean those who are still on this earth at the time of the Second Coming. Since all men are subject to death, the most probable meaning is that they will die and be brought before the judgment seat of Christ in an instant.

The judgment of Christ will bring to light who has believed and lived the Gospel and who has not. The Gospels make it clear that the believer has already been judged favorably and so has nothing whatever to fear from the particular or general judgment. The particular judgment will give confirmation to the individual that he or she is saved, while the general judgment will be a public manifestation of the power and the glory of Christ.

In the Creed, the explicit reference is only to the general or Last Judgment. The Church also teaches, in the Council of Florence (1439), that the particular judgment of the individual follows soon after his death.

A great deal of mystery surrounds our personal existence as human beings, our origin and our destiny. We did not ask to be created, nor did God ask us. Out of pure love, he created us and endowed us with many gifts, both natural and supernatural. Like the steward in the Gospel who must give an accounting of his stewardship, we must give an accounting to God. The final scrutiny will center around our faith and our love—both of God and man. Jesus is our model for both. He also has left us a graphic description of the Last Judgment in Matthew (25:31–46).

29

JESUS' ETERNAL KINGDOM

In the Nicene Creed we profess our belief in the eternal kingdom of Jesus when we say: "His kingdom will have no end." Though we modern Americans have not had the experience of a kingdom and kings, we know what it is from our study of history and from the fact that there are still a few kings left in the world.

There is no doubt that Jesus is a king. In reply to Pilate's questioning as to whether or not he was a king, Jesus said, "You say that I am a king" (Jn 18:37). He was put to death for claiming to be a king, for the inscription put over his Cross, giving the reason for his crucifixion, read, "Jesus of Nazareth, King of the Jews". And recall what the good thief said just in time to steal heaven: "Jesus, remember me when you come into your kingdom" (Lk 23:42).

So Jesus was and is a king. If we reflect for a moment on the content of the preaching of Jesus in Galilee and Judea, we will note that it began with the proclamation of the kingdom of God (or of heaven in Matthew) and that the theme of the kingdom pervades the Gospels all the way to Calvary itself. Jesus began his public life with the plea: "The time is fulfilled, and the kingdom of God is at hand" (Mk 1:15).

A king is a ruler of a people and a ruler is one who has authority over others. "Kingdom" can be understood in two different ways: 1) it can mean the territory over which the king rules, or 2) it can mean the power or "reign" of the king over his people. When we speak of the "kingdom of God", we are using the word "kingdom" primarily in the second sense.

Thus the expression "kingdom of God" refers to the reign of God over the minds and hearts of the elect, of his faithful people. The kingdom itself is a mysterious reality. It is also a growing thing—it is not yet totally complete. It is in the process of being finally established. This idea is brought out by the many beautiful parables of the kingdom that Our Lord used in his instruction of the people. Thus he says that the kingdom of heaven is like a man who sowed good seed in his field; it is like a grain of mustard seed; it is like leaven that is hidden in dough, like a treasure hidden in a field, like a merchant in search of fine pearls who finds one of great value, like a net thrown into the sea (see Mt 13).

The parables, which express a *growth* of the kingdom, apply to the reign of Christ in the Church now. They allow for a delay between the historical beginning of the kingdom during the life of Jesus, which is now being continued by the Church through the preaching of the Word and the administration of the sacraments, and its full realization and manifestation at the end of the world when Jesus will come again in glory to judge the living and the dead.

In God's good time, world history will come to an end and the power of his grace will become manifest. Those who have died in God's grace will enter into his kingdom that will never end. Jesus' kingdom will be eternal because he is eternal and those who are saved will share in his eternal life.

No one except the Father knows when the final, eschatological kingdom will be established (see Acts 1:6–7). Accordingly, all are to watch and to wait and to be ready at any moment for the coming of the kingdom, for it will come "like a thief in the night" for those who believe there is nothing to fear. In fact, the coming of the kingdom is an object of hope and desire for those who love the Lord. For, every time we pray the Our Father we beseech the Lord: "Thy kingdom come."

30

THE HOLY SPIRIT:
LORD AND GIVER OF LIFE

The Nicene Creed is divided into three main parts, one part being dedicated to each of the three divine Persons—Father, Son and Holy Spirit. So far we have dealt with the Father and the Son, Jesus Christ our Lord. It remains for us to consider our profession of faith in the Holy Spirit and the Church which he animates.

Of the three divine Persons, the most mysterious one and the most difficult one for us to think about is the Holy Spirit. We can think about God the Father as the source of all things. We can even imagine him as a kindly and merciful Father. In the case of Jesus, we are dealing with a man like us who lived almost two thousand years ago in Palestine. In the Gospels we find an account of his life and teaching so we can not only think about him, but we can also use our imagination to picture him and to follow him through his earthly life. This is especially true for those who have had the good fortune to visit the Holy Land.

When it comes to the Holy Spirit, however, the matter becomes more difficult. Since the Holy Spirit has not assumed any bodily form, it is impossible for us to imagine him in any concrete way. True, certain symbols are associated with him in Scripture, but they remain mysterious. At his baptism in the Jordan the Spirit of God descended on Jesus in the form of a dove (Mt 3:16). The Spirit is also associated with wind, fire and prophecy (see Acts 2). In Christian art we often see the Holy Spirit represented under these forms. But still it is hard for us to think of the Holy Spirit as a third divine Person distinct from the Father and the Son.

Nevertheless, we know from Scripture, especially from the New Testament, that in addition to the Father and the Son, there is a third divine Person in the unity of the Godhead who is fully divine and equal to the Father and the Son. Scripture calls him the "Spirit", "the Spirit of God", "the Spirit of Jesus", "the Holy Spirit", the "gift" of God, the "advocate". These are some of the titles applied to the third Person of the Blessed Trinity. This truth has been enshrined in the various creeds of the Church and in numerous official documents of the councils of the Church.

So we begin the third part of the Creed by affirming: "I believe in the Holy Spirit, the Lord, the giver of life." The Spirit is called "holy" because he proceeds from the Father and is the source of sanctification in the faithful. The Holy Spirit is also said to be "the Lord". We have already seen that Jesus Christ is called the "one Lord" in the second part of the Creed. Why then use the same title with regard to the Holy Spirit? As was explained in that article, the title "Lord" is an affirmation of divinity, since its application derives from the use of "Yahweh" in the Old Testament. Thus, when the Church applies the title "Lord" to the Holy Spirit, she is saying that the Holy Spirit is truly God, co-equal with the Father and the Son.

We also profess that the Holy Spirit is "the giver of life". For the ancients, breath in the body (which is what "spirit" literally means) was the sign of life. Then it came to mean the source or principle of life. God's Spirit was involved in the production of all life in the world as we read in Genesis (1:2): "The Spirit of God was moving over the face of the waters." It is the Spirit that gives life, both physical and spiritual. In order to have eternal life a man must be born "of water and the Spirit" (Jn 3:5). According to St. Paul, "the Spirit brings life" (2 Cor 3:6). Since it is the Holy Spirit who pours out charity in the hearts of the faithful (Gal 5:5), he is the source of all true life in God. So in the Creed we proclaim our belief that the Holy Spirit is "the giver of life".

31

THE ORIGIN OF THE HOLY SPIRIT

In the Nicene Creed, after professing belief in the Holy Spirit, we go on to say that he "proceeds from the Father and the Son". As we have seen, the Son proceeds from the Father alone who is the originless origin of both the Son and the Holy Spirit.

The idea of "procession" or "coming forth" in the inner divine life has its basis in a number of Scriptural texts. Jesus says of himself in John 8 (42), "For I proceeded and came forth from God"; and he says of the Spirit that he "proceeds from the Father" (Jn 15:26). In these texts Jesus is speaking not only of the external manifestations of the Spirit and his own Incarnation in time and space, but he is also referring to the internal, eternal origin of himself and the Holy Spirit.

By "procession" is understood the origin of one from another. When we speak of an internal, divine procession, we mean the origin of one divine Person from another through the communication of the numerically one divine essence. It is to be remembered that it is not the divine essence or substance that proceeds; rather, the Second Person (Son) proceeds from the originless Father and the Third Person (Holy Spirit) proceeds from the Father and the Son as from one principle. For, the Second Council of Lyons (1274) defined as a dogma of faith that the Holy Spirit proceeds from the Father and the Son, not as from two principles, but as from one principle.

Both Father and Son constitute one principle of the Holy Spirit because the Son, by virtue of his eternal generation from the Father, possesses everything that the Father possesses except the fatherhood. In John 16 (15), Jesus says in testimony of this, "All that the Father has is mine." This means that he must be the principle, along with the Father, of the Holy Spirit.

Let me remind you that we previously spoke about the procession of the Son from the Father. There we said that the Son was "generated" from the Father. Thus there are two processions in the inner divine life of God: the procession of the Son from the Father which we call "generation", and the procession of the Holy Spirit from the Father and the Son as from one principle. Since the Holy Spirit is not "generated" by the Father and the Son, he is not to be called something like a second son of God. Jesus Christ is the "only-begotten Son of God". So there is only one divine Son.

The Fathers of the Church invented a new word to designate the procession of the Holy Spirit. They called it "spiration" or "breathing forth". The word, of course, is related to "spirit" or "breath". The reason for this is that the Holy Spirit proceeds from the will or the mutual love of the Father and the Son. Hence he has a special relationship to love, which is an impulse or impelling of sorts, and which in human persons is manifested by heightened activity—often by an increase in heavy breathing. The connection between the Holy Spirit and love is brought out by St. Paul in Romans (5:5): "The charity of God is poured forth into our hearts by the Holy Spirit, who is given to us."

The essential activities of any spiritual-personal being are knowing and willing. Scripture tells us clearly, and the tradition of the Church from the beginning bears witness to the belief, that there are three Persons in one God. Scripture indicates, and the Fathers and the magisterium of the Church teach, that the procession of the Son is related to God's knowing and the procession of the Holy Spirit is related to God's willing and loving. For this reason the Son is said to be the "wisdom" of God and the Holy Spirit is said to be the "love" or "gift" of God.

Thus the Holy Spirit proceeds from an act of willing in God—the mutual love between the Father and the Son, and so the Nicene Creed professes that he "proceeds from the Father and the Son".

32

WORSHIP OF THE HOLY SPIRIT

There is only one God and to God alone are due glory, worship and adoration. As we have seen, the Nicene Creed, however, proclaims faith in three distinct, not separate, Persons in God: Father, Son and Holy Spirit. We acknowledge God the Father as our Creator and so offer him our praise and adoration. God the Son, incarnate in Jesus of Nazareth, is our Redeemer. We worship him and show him homage—not only in our prayers, but especially in the Blessed Sacrament of the altar.

In the early history of the Church, the question arose about the nature and place of the Holy Spirit who spoke through the prophets, who was active in Jesus during his public life, who descended upon the Apostles at Pentecost and who manifested himself through many marvelous gifts imparted to those who believed in the Lord Jesus and had the hands of the Apostles laid upon their heads.

When theological reflection on Christian revelation began to develop in the third century and afterwards, there was some question as to the divinity and the personality of the Holy Spirit. In order to affirm both of these points the Creed states: "With the Father and the Son he (the Holy Spirit) is worshipped and glorified." So, just as worship and glory are offered by Christians to the Father and the Son, so also are they with perfect right offered to the Holy Spirit. This means then that the Holy Spirit is co-equal with the Father and the Son in divinity and majesty.

It follows then that just as the Father and the Son are divine Persons, subsisting in the one divine substance, so also is the Holy Spirit. One of the clearest indications of this truth in the New Testament is the missionary formula at the conclusion of St. Matthew's Gospel where the three Persons are mentioned and given the same level of dignity: "Go therefore and make disciples of all nations, baptizing them in the name of the Father and of the Son and of the Holy Spirit" (Mt 28:19).

We say in the Creed that we "worship" and "glorify" the Holy Spirit. Worship frequently means "adoration" of God which can be expressed in many different ways: through prayer, sacrifice, solitude, penance. The main idea in adoration is that man, the weak creature, recognizes his creaturehood and therefore his total dependence on almighty God. When we "glorify" God, we praise and give expression to his infinite perfections such as his goodness, power and love. Thus worship and glory are offered to the Holy Spirit in the same sense as they are offered to the Father and the Son.

Thus a number of Catholic truths are expressed in the statement of the Creed. We are proclaiming that the Holy Spirit is truly God, since God alone can be worshipped and glorified by man. Likewise we are stating that the Holy Spirit is co-equal with the Father and the Son. He is the third Person in the Blessed Trinity who has been revealed to us in the Scriptures, especially by the life and teaching of Jesus Christ. He manifested himself in the life of Jesus; Jesus imparted him to his Apostles and to the Church; he has been operative in the Church, sanctifying and encouraging, since Pentecost Sunday.

It used to be said that the Holy Spirit was the "forgotten Person" of the Trinity. The reason for this was that most of the prayers of the Church are directed to either the Father or the Son. Also, the faithful seemed to pray primarily to Jesus or to the Father. Since Vatican Council II there has been a significant change in this regard. More and more Catholics are speaking about the Holy Spirit, praying to him and calling upon him for gifts and illumination. At this period in the history of the Church, the Holy Spirit has come into his own. No longer can he be referred to as the "forgotten Person" in the Blessed Trinity.

Come, Holy Spirit, and fill the hearts of the faithful.

33

THE HOLY SPIRIT AND PROPHECY

The concluding statement of the Nicene Creed about the Holy Spirit is that "He spoke through the prophets." The reference is primarily to the prophets of the Old Testament, including such giants as Isaiah, Jeremiah, Ezekiel, Amos and Hosea.

In the Old Testament a prophet is not primarily one who predicts the future. The idea of a prophet as one who predicts future events is a popular conception that corresponds with only a part of the function of the true prophet. A prophet is simply someone, inspired by God, who speaks in the name of God and who expresses God's commands or his promises.

Certain traits distinguish the prophets of Israel. In the first place, a prophet is constituted by a divine call. This is evident in the call of Isaiah, Jeremiah and Ezekiel (see Is 6:5 ff.; Jer 1:9; Ezek 3:1 ff.). The prophet is always called by God for a religious purpose—he receives a divine mission. That mission is usually to proclaim the Word of God to Israel or to some specific individual, such as Nathan rebuking David for his adultery with Bathsheba (2 Sam 12:1–15).

The true prophets encounter great trials and suffering in the process of bringing the will of God to their fellow men. Jeremiah, conscious of the responsibility of being a prophet, begged God to leave him in peace and to find someone else to do the prophesying (see Jer 1). Under the kings in Israel and Judah the prophets were often executed (Jer 2:30; 26:20–23). Thus Jesus was able to say: "O Jerusalem, Jerusalem, killing the prophets and stoning those who are sent to you. . . ." (Mt 23:37).

In the Old Testament "the Spirit of the Lord" descends on the prophet and he speaks. Thus there is a close association between the Spirit and the human activity of speaking. The prophets counseled the community of Israel, they rebuked her, they denounced the kings and the wealthy oppressors of the poor, they spoke about the "Messiah"—the mysterious anointed king who would one day come to redeem Israel.

In the New Testament Jesus is vividly described in terms that indicate a Spirit-filled prophet who is mighty in word and deed. Although he does not call himself a prophet explicitly, he is referred to by others a number of times as a great prophet from the Lord. The Holy Spirit is active in his conception (Lk 1:35; Mt 1:20), leads him into the desert to be tempted (Lk 4:1) and directs him back to Nazareth, his home town, where he proclaims that the prophecy of Isaiah (61:1–2) is now fulfilled in his own person: "The Spirit of the Lord is upon me, because he has anointed me to preach good news to the poor" (Lk 4:18).

Our forefathers in the early Church composed the Creed. Their faith derived from the preaching of the Apostles. It was the Apostles and the other disciples in the primitive Church who saw that Jesus was the fulfillment of all the prophecies of the Old Testament, a point brought out repeatedly in St. Matthew's Gospel. The prophecies had all come true in Jesus of Nazareth. This meant to them that it was indeed God's Spirit who had spoken through the prophets in the time of Israel before the coming of Jesus Christ. They gave expression to this conviction and this truth by including in their Creed that the Holy Spirit "spoke through the prophets".

34

FAITH IN THE CHURCH

The Nicene Creed embodies our official profession of faith as Roman Catholics. The three major sections concern the Holy Trinity—Father, Son and Holy Spirit. In the final section we profess our faith in the Church, Baptism, resurrection of the dead and eternal life. Let us reflect on our faith in the Church.

If you think about it for a minute, it is truly astonishing that we say we believe in "the Church". Non-Catholic Christians do not look upon the Church as we do. For many of them, the Church is an historical "accident" not intended by Christ—something that just happened after the death of Jesus. They do not look upon the Church as a structured body, a hierarchical institution or a perfect society that was founded by Christ on Peter, the "rock", and intended to perdure until the Second Coming of Jesus in glory.

For the Catholic, however, the Church is all of that and more. The Church is also the pilgrim People of God on its way to the glory of the Father; it is the Mystical Body of Christ—a *body* because it is structured, visible and historical, and *mystical* because it is animated by the Spirit of Jesus Christ; it is the Bride of Christ which he loves and for which he offered his life; it is a holy temple composed of many parts; it is a sacred community, held together by one faith and one Baptism, which operates through the seven sacraments given to her by her Founder.

No matter which image or images are used to describe the Church, none of them is completely adequate because the Church is a "mystery". This means that the total reality of the Church ultimately escapes the confines of human concepts and images. The principle which makes the Church possible in the first place is from above, for the Church is from God and transcends the capacity of the human mind fully to comprehend it.

In early Christian mosaics, the Church was often represented by Noah's ark, the idea being that just as Noah and his family were saved from the flood by the ark, so also the Church is the only "ark" of salvation for us. Thus we find St. Cyprian in the third century saying that "outside the Church there is no salvation," an idea that has been repeated in Church documents since that time (see Vatican II, Constitution on the Church, 14). The formula was narrowly understood by Fr. Leonard Feeney in the late 1940s, but in clarifying the Church's position on the matter the Holy Office in 1949, in a letter that was approved by Pope Pius XII, explained that those who are in a state of invincible ignorance about the necessity of belonging to the Catholic Church can be saved if they have at least an *implicit desire* to enter the Church and if their hearts are informed with *perfect charity* (see *DS* 3866–73).

When we say that "we believe in the Church" we are making the Church an object of supernatural and divine faith. When we believe something by divine faith, this means that we accept it as true on the Word of God himself who has revealed it to us.

Thus the very existence of the Church, including her essential structure and her outstanding characteristics, has been revealed to us by Jesus Christ. Accordingly, we profess our belief in the one Church of Jesus Christ when we pray the Nicene Creed.

Since the Church was founded by Jesus, but on the human foundation of Peter and the other Apostles, it has both divine and human dimensions. Because the Church is also human she has some defects—scandals that sometimes drive people away from her. But we must never forget that, with all the faults of her ministers and people, she is still the only bride of Christ. Above all, she is our mother since she gave us birth into the supernatural life of grace that makes us adopted sons of God and heirs of the kingdom. We not only believe in her; we also love her as the one mother who will never fail us.

35

ONE CHURCH

In contemporary America we are daily confronted with the reality of the Church and the churches. It is an article of Catholic faith that there is only one Church of Jesus Christ—the Church that he founded on Peter and the Apostles and that continues to this very moment only in the Roman Catholic Church. We profess this belief in the Creed when we say, "I believe in one Church."

In our experience, however, we encounter many Christian bodies that claim to be the true Church of Jesus Christ. It has been estimated that there are more than two hundred religious groups in the United States that call themselves Christian. St. Paul said that we are "one body" in Christ, but our painful experience tells us that the body of Christ is divided into many. The causes of these divisions can be found through a careful historical analysis of the beginnings of the various religious bodies.

Many Christian religions do not claim to be the one true Church of Jesus Christ. However, the Roman Catholic Church has claimed at least since the time of

St. Paul that "there is one body and one Spirit, just as you were called to the one hope that belongs to your call, one Lord, one faith, one baptism, one God and Father of us all" (Eph 4:4–6). She claims to be, and we Catholics believe, that she is the one true Church.

When we say that the Catholic Church is "one" we are not only affirming that it is the only true Church of Jesus Christ, and therefore that all the other Christian bodies are defective in some way; we are also saying that the Church is undivided in itself, that it has internal and external unity. Internal or spiritual unity is achieved through the possession of the one Spirit of Christ that he poured out on his Church on Pentecost and continues to pour out on those who believe and receive the sacraments. External unity is attained through unity of doctrine, worship and government. The Catholic Church is one in all three senses because it has a unified hierarchy that is in communion with the Pope, the successor of St. Peter, and is subject to his universal authority or jurisdiction in the Church. Unity of faith, worship and leadership produce one Church.

Other Christian ecclesial bodies have varying degrees of organizational unity, but none of them is a worldwide Church such as the Catholic Church with the same faith, worship and leadership in all parts of the world where the faith can be freely practiced.

Jesus founded one Church, not many churches, when he said "I will build my Church" on Peter, the rock (see Mt 16:18). At the Last Supper he prayed, "that they may be one even as we are one" (Jn 17:11); and again, "that they may all be one even as thou, Father, art in me, and I in thee . . . so that the world may believe that thou hast sent me" (Jn 17:21). The unity of the Catholic Church has been a perpetual source of conversions in the past, since it is obvious to anyone who studies and meditates on the Jesus of the Gospels that he willed only one Church. He bequeathed unity and peace to us, not division and discord. But there is division and discord among Christians—so much so that it is a scandal and seriously obstructs the work of converting the world to Christ. In recent years many Catholics, Protestants and Orthodox Christians have come to the realization that these divisions are the result of sin. The deep desire to restore unity to the divided body of Christ gave birth to the ecumenical movement.

At this stage in history, no one knows how complete unity can be restored. Certainly it will never be accomplished by following the advice of some Catholic intellectuals who seem to be willing to sacrifice truth for the sake of unity. Unity must be based on truth, for unity based on error is no unity at all. We should pray for the unity of all Christians in one Church in the words of Our Lord, "that they may be one".

36

THE CHURCH IS HOLY

The Nicene Creed singles out four characteristics or "marks" by which the true Church of Jesus Christ is recognized. Thus, in the Creed we profess our belief in the "one, holy, catholic and apostolic Church". We have seen that the Church is one. Now let us reflect on the holiness of the Church.

At its root "holiness" means the infinite fullness of the divine being, power and goodness that we are able to grasp in some way through normal human experience. It always remains mysterious to us and so it is ineffable, but at the same time it has a strange fascination. Theologians also speak of the "moral" holiness of God, which means his will, which essentially consists in his love—first of himself and then of all the creatures that he has produced out of nothingness.

Persons and things are said to be "holy" to the extent that they are dedicated to God or related to him and his service in some way. So the notion of holiness belongs primarily to God and only secondarily to creatures.

The Church is the community of all those who have faith in Jesus Christ and possess his Spirit. It is a dogma of our Catholic faith that the Church herself is holy, since her holiness is professed in the Nicene Creed.

The Church is holy in her origin, her purpose, her means and the results she produces. She is holy in her origin since she was founded by Jesus Christ himself and was given the Holy Spirit as her animating principle. In fact, St. Paul says that Jesus is the head of the Church and the members constitute his Body—the Mystical Body of Christ. The Church is also holy in her purpose which is the glory of God and the sanctification and salvation of men.

Certain aspects of the holiness of the Church are visible to those who are willing to look and see. It is this "visible" holiness of the Church that is meant by the holy as a "mark" of the true Church of Jesus Christ.

Thus, the means that the Church uses to attain her goal are holy. They include such things as the Word of God as contained in the Bible which is vastly superior to any philosophy or purely human religion; the Ten Commandments and the evangelical counsels; the liturgy of the sacraments, especially the Holy Sacrifice of the Mass; her laws and institutions, such as the multiplicity of religious orders and congregations; the sacramentals of the Church, devotions and so forth.

The Church is also holy in her fruits, that is, she is known from the holiness of those men and women who, filled with the faith of the Church, make full use of the means of grace and holiness put at their disposal by the Church. These are the "saints" of the Church, both those who have been officially canonized, such as St. Theresa, St. Francis Xavier, St. John Vianney, and those who have died in the grace of God or who, possessing that same grace, are now living holy lives and walking in the paths of the Lord. These are the ones who are "the salt of the earth" (Mt 5:13) and "the light of the world" (Mt 5:14).

The Church, therefore, is not only holy in herself, but she also produces holy men and women, that is, she brings forth "saints". From her holy "fruits" she is seen to be holy and so holiness is one of the marks of the true Church of Jesus Christ.

37

THE CATHOLICITY OF THE CHURCH

The third "mark" of the true Church of Jesus Christ is that she must be "catholic", which means "general" or "universal". The Church founded by Jesus was called "catholic" in the first third of the second century by some of the early Fathers of the Church, such as St. Ignatius of Antioch and St. Polycarp. It began appearing in various creeds towards the end of the second century and has been in the Nicene Creed since the fourth century. So, that the Church of Jesus Christ is "catholic" is an article of faith and is to be believed by all.

The universality of God's salvific will for all men was suggested in the Old Testament, but does not come to full fruition until God establishes a new and eternal covenant with man in Jesus Christ. St. Paul says that "God desires all men to be saved and to come to the knowledge of the truth" (1 Tim 2:4). Before ascending into heaven, Jesus commanded his Apostles: "Go therefore and make disciples of all nations, baptizing them in the name of the Father and of the Son and of the Holy Spirit" (Mt 28:19; also Mk 16:15; Acts 1:8).

The catholicity of the Church has both an external and an internal dimension. *Externally*, it means that the Church is a unified body that authentically derives from Jesus Christ who founded her and is both basically and actually spread throughout the world. *Internally*, it means that the Church of Christ is endowed with all of the supernatural means (Gospel, grace, sacraments) necessary to effect the eternal salvation of all people at all times and in every land.

Since the time of the Apostles to the present day, the only Christian Church that claims to be "catholic" in the sense described is the Holy Roman Catholic Church. In fact, the notion of catholicity is so important that it is included in the very name of the Roman Church. She is the parent Church from which all other Christian churches derive. It is for this reason that the Second Vatican Council says that the "unique Church of Christ" "*subsists* in the Catholic Church" (Constitution on the Church, 8). By this expression, the Council affirmed that the fullness of the Church of Christ was to be found only in the Roman Catholic Church, while various "elements" of sanctification and truth can be found in other Christian confessions. In fact, the Fathers of the Church used the word "catholic" to designate the true Church of Christ in opposition to the heretical or schismatic sects which were narrowly and locally confined. Thus, universality was seen as a mark of the true Church. What was true in the third century is still true in the twentieth.

The Church is universal or catholic in the sense that she was destined by Christ himself for all men of all times and places. Seen in this light, the Church can be said to be qualitatively universal. But that would not be much if the Church were not in some sense quantitatively or actually universal. St. Paul even in his day (c. 58 A.D.) could speak of the faith as being known throughout the whole world (Rom 1:8). That is more true today than ever before. The faith of the Church has been planted in all continents and among all the major peoples of the world. At one time the Church flourished in North Africa; now she is expanding rapidly in sub-Saharan Africa. The success of the faith varies according to time and place. But when the Lord deigns to come again in glory to judge the world, he will find that his Apostles and the bishops, their successors, have carried out his mandate to preach the Gospel "to all nations".

38

THE CHURCH IS APOSTOLIC

According to our traditional faith, as expressed in the Nicene Creed, we believe in the "apostolic Church". The distinguishing note of apostolicity was added to the Creed in the fourth century.

The apostolicity of the Church means the essential identity everywhere and since the time of her foundation with the Church of the Apostles. Thus the Church that has remained faithful to what the Apostles founded and bequeathed to their successors is by that very fact "apostolic". It follows also from this that such a Church is also the true Church of Jesus Christ since he is the "cornerstone". St. Paul says that the Church was "built on the foundation of the Apostles and prophets, Christ Jesus himself being the cornerstone" (Eph 2:20).

The apostolicity of the Church is manifested in three ways: 1) apostolic origin, that is, the Church was founded by Christ on the Apostles and especially through them;

2) the apostolic doctrine, that is, the identity of faith with that preached by the Apostles; 3) the apostolic succession, that is, the uninterrupted chain of legitimate bishops who link the Church of the Apostles with the Church of today.

The only Church today that manifests the fullness of apostolicity is the Holy Roman Catholic Church. The Protestant churches lack the apostolic origin, since they did not appear until the sixteenth century. They are also defective in the doctrine of the Apostles and they do not have the necessary apostolic succession.

The situation of the Eastern Orthodox churches is different. They do have the apostolic succession of their bishops, going back to the Apostles, but they are defective in some teachings and, especially, they have broken communion with the pope, who is the legitimate successor of St. Peter and the source of unity in the Church.

The Catholic Church claims to be "apostolic" in a unique sense that applies to her alone. She alone claims to possess, in the person of our Holy Father in Rome, the power of the keys that Our Lord promised to St. Peter and conferred on him. She has always acted in this confidence. This belief is emblazoned in marble wherever you look, both inside and outside, in St. Peter's Basilica in Rome.

Apostolicity roots the Church in space and time. She can never abandon it as a criterion of the true Church, otherwise, as Karl Rahner has aptly said, "instead of being a tangible, historical reality the Church would be an abstract idea."

The four notes of unity, sanctity, catholicity and apostolicity are not just hidden characteristics; they are external, recognizable marks of the true Church of Christ. Under Pope Pius IX the Holy Office declared: "The true Church of Christ, by virtue of divine authority, is constituted and is knowable by the four characteristics, which we confess in the Creed as an object of the faith" (*DS* 2888).

39

BAPTISM AND
THE FORGIVENESS OF SINS

Towards the end of the Nicene Creed we say: "We acknowledge one baptism for the forgiveness of sins." We all know what Baptism is and what it effects in the recipient, but it might be well to recall some of the truths associated with this life-giving rite.

Baptism is closely associated with the life of Jesus on earth. He personally received the Baptism of John (Mt 3:13–17). While conversing with Nicodemus, Jesus spoke of Baptism as a "new birth" and said that this new birth is necessary if one wishes to enter the kingdom of God (Jn 3:1–5). After his Resurrection Jesus commanded his Apostles to go into the whole world and make disciples of all nations and "baptize them in the name of the Father and of the Son and of the Holy Spirit" (Mt 28:19).

The normal person to receive Baptism is the adult who has heard the Gospel and has come to believe that Jesus Christ is the Lord. The basic dispositions necessary to receive Christian Baptism fruitfully are faith and sorrow for one's sins. St. Peter concluded his sermon on the first Pentecost with the admonition that his hearers should believe in the Good News, "repent" and "be baptized in the name of Jesus Christ for the forgiveness of your sins" (Acts 2:38).

All are reminded that the Baptism of infants is the exception rather than the rule in the history of the Church. The infant has no personal sins (only original sin) for which to repent; but he or she must have faith in some way. Catholic teaching stresses that the faith of the Church supplies for the child until it is able to make an act of faith on its own.

The effect of Baptism is a "new birth" for the human person into the supernatural life of grace. By his "rebirth" the new Christian takes on a new mode of being; he now becomes a spiritual person; he is incorporated into the community of believers, which is the Church; God's life now dwells in him and he has a claim to see God forever in heaven; God infuses into his soul the supernatural virtues of faith, hope and charity. As a result of this "rebirth", all sins are remitted by God—this includes original sin and all personal sins, plus the temporal punishment in purgatory due to them. The soul is washed clean and becomes as white as snow. It is because Baptism by itself remits all sins that we say in the Creed that we acknowledge one Baptism "for the forgiveness of sins".

When we say that we acknowledge *one* Baptism we are giving affirmation to the infallible teaching of the

Church that valid Baptism imprints on the soul of the recipient an indelible spiritual mark—called the baptismal "character"—and thus cannot be repeated. In the early Church some thought that Baptism by heretics was invalid; others thought that if a person fell into mortal sin he would have to be rebaptized when he repented. The Magisterium of the Church rejected these opinions as false and has taught ever since that a valid Baptism can never be repeated. Thus, Christians validly baptized in an Orthodox or Protestant church, when they convert to Catholicism, are not to be rebaptized. They are required to receive the Sacrament of Penance and to make a profession of Catholic faith.

40

THE RESURRECTION OF THE DEAD

Resurrection means the return of a dead man to life. When we say at the conclusion of the Nicene Creed that "we look for the resurrection of the dead" we are making a profession of faith in a great mystery that only God himself can reveal and carry out.

In the Old Testament there was a gradual development of the belief in the resurrection which reached its highpoint in the prophet Daniel and in 2 Maccabees. In New Testament times the idea was rejected by the Sadducees—those constant opponents of Jesus. They were crass materialists who believed only in the here and now. In our own day by logical necessity all rationalists, materialists and atheists must, if they are true to their own principles, reject the notion of resurrection of the dead as absurd. They must reject it because it is so clearly beyond all human powers. Thus, if there is a resurrection, there must be a God who effects it, and they will not admit that.

Jesus clearly taught the resurrection of the dead in the Gospels. This doctrine is a favorite theme of St. John and also of St. Paul who gives it extensive treatment in 1 Corinthians (15).

The "resurrection of the dead" professed in the Creed will take place at the end of the world—a time, unknown to anyone except the Father (Mk 13:32), when this whole changing world as we know it will be transformed by the power of God into something completely new. That is the moment when Jesus will come again in his glory and will judge the living and the dead. This event is also known as the "Parousia" of the Lord.

If the "resurrection" means the return to life of the dead, what kind of life will it be? It will be a life of supreme joy and happiness for those who have died in the love of God and are saved. A point to stress here is that the joy of the saved affects not just the soul, but the whole person of body and soul. For, at the resurrection, the soul will be reunited to the body which will share in and reflect the glory of the soul. Also, it is a defined teaching of the Fourth Lateran Council (1215) that the dead will rise with the same body they had on earth. Since all of the matter in our bodies changes about every five years, obviously we will not have exactly the same matter or molecules that we had in time, but we will look the same and we will retain our sexual differentiation.

How many of us really "expect" or "look forward to" the resurrection? The word in the Creed implies a certain longing in the Christian for the end of the world and the Second Coming of Christ—a time when all suffering, evil and death will be wiped away for the redeemed.

Our concern here is primarily with the saved, but it is also Catholic teaching that "all" the dead will rise again —both the saved and the damned. This teaching is based on the clear words of Jesus (Mt 10:28; Jn 5:29). Thus the damned will suffer in hell both in soul and in body.

Jesus himself is the "first fruits" from the dead, as St. Paul said. Our Blessed Mother has also been assumed body and soul into heaven. Jesus has set the pattern for us. This means that we will be transformed into a glory similar to his. In the past, theologians have distinguished four qualities of resurrected bodies. They are: 1) the incapability of suffering or dying; 2) the spiritualization of the body so that it is no longer subject to the laws of nature as it now is; 3) agility, or the capability of the body to obey the soul with the greatest ease and speed of movement; 4) perfection of radiance and beauty.

To unbelievers the resurrection of the dead is foolishness. But to those of us who believe in God and in his infallible Word, the resurrection of Jesus, who said "I am the Resurrection" (Jn 11:25), is the pledge of our own personal resurrection and liberation from the iron jaws of death and corruption.

41

THE LIFE OF THE WORLD TO COME

The Nicene Creed concludes with a strong note of hope —hope for the resurrection of the dead and "the life of the world to come". In this final essay on the Creed we will reflect for a few moments on the meaning of "eternal life".

From our own experience we all know what life is. It is the supreme good in this world—something we strive to preserve at all cost. Men and women will give up their wealth and undergo the most painful operations and treatments in order to sustain their lives a few more months or years. And constantly we live in the shadow of death—the all-consuming, rapacious, inescapable jaws that eventually devour each one of us.

From physical death, and the personal disintegration that it connotes, we hope to escape by entering into eternal life. By his death and Resurrection Jesus was victorious over death. All those who enter into his life-death-Resurrection by faith, Baptism and the exercise of the theological virtues of faith, hope and charity, are summoned by the Father to be participators with Christ in the eternal kingdom.

By faith we know that in addition to our material-biological life on earth there is another, higher life of grace that is open to all who believe in the Father, in Jesus Christ his only Son, and in the Holy Spirit. The supernatural life of grace is an unmerited, total gift of God which begins in this life by faith and Baptism and is brought to completion in "the world to come" when the veils of this flesh are removed so that we can see God as he is, face to face.

Our infallible Catholic faith teaches us that our life does not cease at death. In the preface of the Mass for the Dead the Church prays that in death life is not extinguished but only changed into a new, permanent, glorious kind of life.

We pray in the Creed that we are looking for the life "of the world to come". There are many Scriptural overtones in this expression. We know from our faith that one day God will destroy the present world. This means that one day there will be an end to conception, life, growth and death. The New Testament writers speak of the "new heaven and the new earth" that God is going to fashion. What this new heaven and earth will be like and how God will accomplish his plan, he has not seen fit to reveal to us.

God's purpose in creating the universe, the human race and each human person, is that we might share in his abundant life. That is the end that he intends for each and every one of us.

Thus, God desires that all men be saved and that all come to a knowledge of the truth (1 Tim 2:4). However, in order to attain the permanent divine life that he has in store for us, he demands that we freely love him in return for his many kindnesses to us. And the way we show that we love God is by keeping his commandments (Jn 14:15).

Accordingly, we see that there is a well thought out plan in the Creed: it moves from the Father, to the Son, to the Holy Spirit, to the Church and finally to the "last things"—especially the resurrection and eternal life.

It is one thing to be able to recite the Nicene Creed with understanding at Sunday Mass; it is something else to live our Catholic lives in the full realization and implementation of the Creed. In these short essays on the Creed I have tried to convey more knowledge about the essentials of our Catholic faith. Knowledge is not the same thing as faith, but it is an essential part of it. Our Lord himself said: "This is eternal life: to know you, the only true God, and Jesus Christ whom you have sent" (Jn 17:3).

PART II

THE COMMANDMENTS

I

FAITH AND MORALITY

As St. James insists, faith without works is dead. It is not enough just to shout "Lord, Lord" in order to please God and to be saved. One must not only believe with one's mind and heart what God has revealed in order to be saved. One must also do the will of God in ordinary, everyday living. According to the way man has been created by God (which reflects the order of being in God himself), reasonable actions—worthy of a human being—always flow from thought. As we think, so we act. If a person thinks that good manners are not important, that person will tend to be discourteous and act like a "slob".

Hence, now that we have reflected on the essentials of the Catholic faith, the next step is to go on to a consideration of the implications of that faith for my relationships with others—with God and with my fellow men. In the whole field of Catholic theology this practical part of it has been called "Moral Theology" for about four hundred years. Currently moral theology is often called "Christian morality" or "Christian ethics".

Morality is concerned with what is good for man in the domain of personal relations with others. The word "morality" is derived from the Latin *mores* which means the customs or habitual ways of acting of a tribe or group of human beings that live together. The assumption has been made, and not without foundation in objective reality, that the recognized and time-tried customs of a cohesive human group are valid standards of action and that they correspond to the demands of truth and of the Supreme Being. Thus, a person who allowed himself to be guided by these customs was thought to be moral. The person who refused to live by these standards was said to be immoral. The study of morality, then, is concerned with the norms of human activity. It seeks to discern what the truly good is for man in all situations of life. Since the good is what makes a person happy, if he or she can find the norms of a good life, and then follows them, that person will have a reasonably happy life. On the other hand, rejection of good morals leads to unhappiness.

As should also be evident, good morality on the part of the citizens of a state contributes to the harmonious living together of those citizens. It stands to reason that if the citizens of a given state do not lie, cheat, steal, kill, rape, etc., the daily lives of those citizens will proceed in peace and tranquility.

For the Catholic Christian good morality is more than common sense; it is more than the results of philosophical or anthropological inquiries. For the Catholic, morality flows from the very faith that he professes in Jesus Christ. Jesus did not just teach abstract doctrines about his Father and the Holy Spirit, about heaven and hell. He did that, certainly, but he also taught us how to live. An excellent summary of what Jesus thought about the good life is found in his Sermon on the Mount in Matthew 5.

And Jesus did more than just teach his Apostles the principles of a holy life. He first lived that life himself. Jesus incarnated in his Person the perfection of all the moral virtues. It is for this reason that Jesus Christ is the model of all Christian living. By modeling their own lives on Jesus' life, the saints became saints.

Jesus taught us both by his words and by his deeds. He is the concrete model of all Christian living. Thus, Christian morality is based on the words and deeds of Jesus. In the following essays I plan to consider the basic principles of Christian morality and to give a brief exposition of the content, meaning and implications of the Ten Commandments. There is much confusion today about the moral teaching of the Catholic Church. I intend to detail the fundamentals of Catholic morality as they are found in the teaching of the Church and in the writings of theologians who are loyal to the Magisterium of the Church.

2

WHAT MAKES HUMAN ACTS GOOD OR BAD?

Man achieves his eternal destiny and eternal salvation by doing good and avoiding evil. Jesus said, "If you love me, keep my commandments." It is easy to establish the general principle of doing good and avoiding evil; it is not so easy in every circumstance, here and now, to know what is good and what is evil.

But there are some basic principles of Christian morality that all Catholics should be familiar with. One of the very first is that any act of a human person must be a conscious, human act before it can have any moral quality whatsoever. A human act is one that proceeds from knowledge and free will. If either adequate knowledge or freedom is lacking in the act of a person, then that act is not fully human and therefore not fully moral. Thus, digestion, growth, the movement of blood in the veins, etc., since they are not under the control of our will, are not spoken of as moral acts at all. They are acts of a human person, but they are not called "human acts".

A fully human act, that is, one proceeding from knowledge and free will, is either morally good or morally evil. How do we know whether a given human act is good or evil? Over the centuries moral theologians have agreed that there are three determinants of the moral quality of our actions. The three are: the object, the circumstances and the intention.

The *object* is the thing with which the action is essentially concerned, for example, lying, praying the rosary, stealing, helping a blind person across the street. For a morally good act, the object of it must be good, that is, the thing with which the action is concerned must conform to the law of God.

The *circumstances* of the act are the second determinant of the morality of any action. The circumstances are such things as the person involved, the time, the place, the occasion, which are distinct from the object, but can change or completely alter its moral tone. Circumstances can make an otherwise good action evil, as when a soldier on guard duty deliberately goes to sleep. They can increase the guilt, as when a girl lies to her mother; or minimize the guilt, as an unpremeditated lie in order to get out of an embarrassing situation. Since all human actions occur at a certain time and at a certain place, the circumstances must always be considered in evaluating the moral quality of any human act.

The third determinant of the moral quality of any human act is the *intention* or *end* or *purpose*. Every human act, no matter how trivial, is done for some purpose. The Sunday driver who blocks traffic and seems to be driving aimlessly has a purpose: he may not be going anywhere definite but he does seek the joy of just driving around and looking. For a human act to be morally good the agent or doer must have a good intention—he must want to accomplish something that is good in one way or another. Some actions, like blasphemy and stealing, are always wrong and no purpose, no matter how noble, can make them good. Other actions may be either good or bad, depending on why we do them. Taking a drink is not sinful; drinking in order to get drunk is. The morality of many things that we do is determined by the intention—such as walking, talking, reading, and so forth. Many such activities are said to be indifferent morally in themselves, but they receive their moral quality from the intention behind them.

For our actions to be good our intention must be good. It is good to help the poor, but if I donate to the poor out of vanity or from revenge, then it is not a good act even though, incidentally, the poor are helped. On the other hand, we must avoid the common contemporary error of thinking that the whole morality of any action is determined by the intention. The most noble intention cannot make an intrinsically evil action a good action. Thus, the bombings and killings perpetrated by terrorists in order to change some form of government are still murder. Stealing from the rich in order to help the poor à la Robin Hood is still stealing. The idea that "the end justifies the means" is very common today. Good but ill-advised people who are concerned about over-population or the proper raising of children resort to abortion in order to cut down the number of births and to avoid unwanted children. But a good intention, no matter what it is, does not make something essentially evil, such as abortion, into something morally good.

We have reason to be alarmed at the increased use of the principle that "the end justifies the means." As well instructed Catholics we should know that the morality of every human act is determined by the object, the circumstances and the intention. If any one of the three is evil, then the human act in question is evil and should be avoided.

3

MORAL RESPONSIBILITY

A fundamental difference between a human person and a tree or a cow is that the person is held responsible for his actions (at least some of them), while the tree and the cow are not said to be responsible for their actions. Both plants and animals act in certain ways by necessity, since they function according to the nature that God endowed them with. Human persons also have a nature, but specifically human actions proceed from knowledge and freedom.

"Responsibility", therefore, is essentially related to free actions that proceed from adequate knowledge. It is clearly recognized both in ethics and in law that a mentally deranged person is not responsible for his or her actions. When we say that a man is responsible for his actions we mean that he knew what he was doing and that he acted freely.

Very closely related to the notion of responsibility is the idea of "imputability", which means that one may be declared the free author of an action and may be held responsible for it. The more free an action is, the more imputable it is, and vice versa. Thus, when we speak about moral responsibility and imputability we are touching on something that is at the very heart of all moral activity.

Since a person can act with more or less knowledge and with more or less freedom, it follows that any restriction on knowledge or freedom will also affect the personal responsibility or imputability of the act. Since man is very limited and is open to a number of influences, we find that there are many obstacles or impediments to fully human acts—all of which affect moral responsibility in one way or another.

Some of the factors that can diminish or altogether remove imputability are: ignorance, emotion or passion, fear, bad habits, violence, hypnosis, drugs and mental illness. All of these affect either a person's mind or his will, or both, and to the extent that they do, they lessen responsibility.

Thus, in the realm of morality a person is not held responsible for the observance of laws that he does not know about. Moralists make a distinction between ignorance that cannot be overcome and ignorance that can be eliminated with minimal effort. The former is called "invincible ignorance"; the latter is called "vincible ignorance". If I am invincibly ignorant of some obligation, such as attending Mass on a Holy Day of obligation, then I am not responsible for missing Mass on that day. Vincible ignorance can be cleared up if one wants to; if I fail to clear it up and thereby violate the law of God, my guilt depends on the degree of neglect involved in persisting in my "voluntary" ignorance.

It is common knowledge and experience that emotions can inhibit clear thinking and free choosing. Sometimes they can be so strong that they remove all culpability. Fear is mental anxiety because of impending evil. It is rarely so strong as to deprive a person of all moral responsibility for actions performed. Fear can lessen imputability but it can also increase the merit involved in good actions when one persists in good in spite of great fear. Such would be the case for a police officer who, in spite of great danger to himself, overcomes his own fear in order to rescue someone held as hostage in a bank robbery.

Violence, bad habits, hypnosis, mental illness, etc. either diminish moral responsibility or totally erase it depending on their influence on the mind and will. Of course, if a person is freely responsible for positing an obstacle to his own knowledge or freedom, such as deliberately getting drunk or taking drugs, then he is fully responsible for what is done or omitted.

In all of this it is important to remember that complete responsibility for human acts depends on their proceeding from adequate knowledge and full consent of the will. Defects not traceable to personal fault will either diminish or totally remove all moral responsibility.

4

DIGNITY OF THE LAW

Moralists emphasize that there are two fundamental norms of morality to which all others can be reduced in one way or another. One of these norms is said to be "objective" and the other is said to be "subjective". The objective norm of morality is law, in all of its ramifications, and the subjective norm of morality is what we call "conscience". In this essay we will consider some aspects of law; in the following essay we will go into the matter of conscience.

Today "law" in America does not have the respect of the people that it once enjoyed. There are many reasons for this development—permissiveness, materialistic atheism, wrongdoing on the part of lawmakers and law enforcers. Many scholars trace a change in the attitude of the American people to law as a result of the fiasco with regard to prohibition in the 1920s. Some recent decisions of our courts in favor of abortion on demand, pornography and so forth, have also eroded respect for the law in religious, usually law-abiding citizens.

When we talk about law it is good to know exactly what we are talking about. The best definition of law was given by St. Thomas Aquinas. He said that law is "an ordinance of reason for the common good, made by him who has care of the community, and promulgated" (*Summa Theologica*, I–II, q. 90, art. 4). The definition contains four basic elements that are common to all true laws: 1) reason; 2) the common good; 3) lawmaking authority, and 4) promulgation. Any discussion of law by a Catholic moralist will make use of this definition in one way or another.

The highest law of all is the *eternal law* which is God's divine plan by which all created things are directed from all eternity to one supreme end. This eternal law is in the mind of God and actually identified with God. The eternal law is made known in time in many different ways, for example, in the physical laws of nature, in the natural moral law (through the function of conscience), in positive divine law through revelation. God makes his will known immediately through human positive laws, whether civil laws or ecclesiastical laws.

There are those today who, hostile to the very notion of law, claim that the Christian is not bound by the Ten Commandments or by other laws. The supreme law for the Christian, they say, is the law of love: love of God and love of one's fellow man. Often they will quote, or misquote, that famous saying of St. Augustine: "Love, and do what you will."

The main difficulty with the "love" position—a position that has attracted many followers—is that it is contrary to the express teaching of Scripture, to the tradition of the Church and even to common sense. Our Lord said on more than one occasion, "If you love me, keep my commandments." He told the rich young man who asked him what he had to do to be saved, "Keep the commandments." When St. Paul spoke against the Jewish "Law", he was not talking about the law of God and the law of nature expressed in the Mosaic law. He was talking about the perverted and inhuman legalism of the scribes and pharisees. Nowhere does he say or imply that the Christian, who is by grace free from the burden of the juridical and ceremonial requirements of the Old Law, is not bound to keep the Ten Commandments.

The law of God, the laws of nature and good human positive laws are all reflections of the eternal law which is in God himself. To the extent that they manifest, in some way or other, the divine plan for mankind, they are good and holy. They point the way to human fulfillment and happiness and ultimately to eternal salvation.

"God desires the salvation of all men and that all come to a knowledge of the truth" (1 Tim 2:4). One of the basic ways in which God reveals himself to us is through his holy law. We see it daily in the laws of nature; we sense it in ourselves in our perception of the basic requirements of the moral law to do good and avoid evil; we hear it preached to us through the ministry of the Church which has been commissioned by Jesus Christ himself to preach the saving law of the Gospel.

Certainly the law can be abused by wicked men. But that does not mean that all law is to be repudiated. On the human level we need good laws, in conformity with the eternal law, framed and promulgated by good and wise men. Legitimate Church laws must be respected and obeyed. Jesus was obedient to his Father; as a result he accomplished our redemption and is glorified at the right hand of the Father. We can do no better than to follow the example of Jesus.

5

THE IDEAL CONSCIENCE: CORRECT AND CERTAIN

Conscience is the supreme subjective norm of morality. We have already considered "law" as the basic objective norm. Today "conscience" is frequently appealed to as an absolutely autonomous principle in a person—as something that is not supposed to be challenged or questioned by anyone, including the Church or the state. In order to deal with this situation it is important to know precisely what conscience is and what it is not.

First, what conscience is not. It is not an "inner voice" telling me what is right and what is wrong. It is not an emotional feeling produced by my parents or by toilet training or by my peer group. Finally, it is not a special faculty, distinct from my mind and my will, that tells me what to do and what to avoid.

According to constant Catholic tradition, especially as it was elaborated by St. Thomas Aquinas, "conscience" is a function of the human intellect making moral judgments. To be more specific, when the mind judges, on the basis of general principles (such as "Thou shalt not steal"), that a particular action should be done or avoided, here and now, then that practical judgment of the mind is called "conscience". Through reason and revelation the mind is conscious of many general, abstract principles, such as the Ten Commandments or the most general moral principle of all, "Do good and avoid evil." Since man lives in time and space and must make decisions all day long in the here and now, he is constantly applying those general principles to concrete situations. The application by the mind of those general principles to concrete cases is what Catholic moralists mean by "conscience".

Conscience both precedes and follows concrete moral actions. Antecedently, conscience will urge me to do some good action or to avoid some evil action. The judgment of conscience following an action is either approving (when the action was good) or condemning (when the action was bad); the latter is said to be a "bad conscience" and is accompanied with a sense of guilt.

Since conscience involves a judgment, it is said to be *correct* when the judgment corresponds with the objective norms of morality; it is said to be *erroneous* when it is not. Subjectively, a conscience is said to be *certain* if an individual has no doubts about the morality of what he is doing; it is said to be *doubtful* if a person is undecided about what to do. The ideal conscience, the one that is to be striven for, is a conscience that is *both correct and certain*.

"Let your conscience be your guide," we say. That is true. The ultimate guide for each person in his moral decisions is his conscience. We must follow the dictates of a certain conscience—even if it is erroneous. However, we may never act with a doubtful conscience. To do so would be equivalent to affirming that we are willing to do something evil. If we are in doubt, therefore, we must either refrain from acting or resolve the doubt. Doubts can be resolved by reflection, by consulting knowledgeable persons like confessors or teachers, by consulting reliable books. Since each person must follow his or her own conscience, it is crucial that one's conscience be correctly formed.

What I want to stress here is the importance of the *formation of conscience*. Conscience does not just happen—it is formed by parents, peer group, school, church, media. In previous ages the principal agents in the formation of conscience of youth were the family, the Church and the school. That is not the case any more. They are still a factor, but it seems to me that, in this electronic, permissive age, the peer group and the media are more effective in the formation of conscience than are the family and the Church.

Since man is fallible and prone to error, it follows that he can err in the matter of conscience. A person may think that he is justified in perpetrating an act of terrorism, he might even be sincere, but that does not make terror and murder good. Today, due to philosophical currents of subjectivism and relativism, many persons tend to absolutize the individual conscience. They neglect the objective principles of morality and claim that an action is good or bad simply because they think it is good or bad. Some of the results of this mentality are a breakdown in public morality, increased violence in our streets, premarital sex, shoplifting, and so forth.

Let me conclude by saying that as Catholics we should cultivate not only a good moral conscience, but also *a Christian conscience*—which is something much more. In addition to reason, we have the added advantage of grace—personal grace, revelation, the teaching of the Church and the good example of the saints. We should learn to judge all things in the light of salvation offered to us in Jesus Christ. He is the model and the examplar, for he is "the way and the truth and the life".

6

TRUE MORALITY IS BASED ON OBJECTIVE PRINCIPLES

One aspect of Catholic moral teaching that distinguishes it from most other moral systems, whether liberal Protestant or secular humanist, is its emphasis on the objectivity of moral principles. For the Catholic Church, the basic principles of morality are God-given, imbedded in human nature, recognizable by human reason and valid for all men of all times.

By her emphasis on the objectivity of moral principles the Church comes into direct conflict with most of the intellectual currents of the day. You have heard of "situation ethics", "existential ethics" and "the new morality". These tags refer to moral systems that are based on the relativity of values. What they say in the concrete is that any act, no matter what it is—stealing, adultery, fornication, murder, terrorism—can be just and good depending on the intention of the perpetrator and the circumstances of the act.

All such subjective moral positions deny that there is a fixed order in nature, given to it by God, that is binding always and everywhere. Current views of permissive sex are merely an amplification of situation ethics. According to situation ethics, all human acts are basically indifferent—they are neither good nor evil in themselves. Their morality, they say, depends on the situation or circumstances. This is a very convenient system for the human ego, for what it means is that the individual at all times decides for himself what is good and what is bad. He recognizes, therefore, no "objective" moral principles.

The Catholic Church has consistently and continually rejected subjectivism and relativism in morality. In one of her recent official documents, the Church stated: "Now in fact the Church throughout her history has always considered a certain number of precepts of the natural law as having an absolute and immutable value, and in their transgression she has seen a contradiction of the teaching and spirit of the Gospel" (*Declaration on Certain Questions Concerning Sexual Ethics*, 4, December 29, 1975). Similar official statements of the Magisterium have been a regular part of Catholic teaching for centuries.

The eternal law of God, as reflected in human nature, is called the "natural moral law". Certain aspects of it, such as the prohibitions against stealing, lying and murder, are easily recognizable by all who are of sound mind. The Greeks and Romans were highly developed in certain parts of the natural law. There is a remarkable reflection of it in the moral system elaborated by Confucius of China twenty-four hundred years ago—a system still followed by millions of Chinese.

However, most men and women do not have the mental acumen of an Aristotle, a Cicero or a Confucius. Frankly, they need help. Now God in his goodness has seen fit to reveal to man, through the prophets of the Old Testament and especially through his Son, Jesus Christ, in the New Testament, the basic requirements of the natural law in addition to the special law of the Gospel. According to Vatican Council I, God did this so that "those religious truths which are by their nature accessible to human reason can easily be known by all men with solid certitude and with no trace of error" (*DS* 3005).

Throughout both Jewish and Christian history the best compendium of God's law for man, of what God expects of man in his daily intercourse with others, has been thought to be the Ten Commandments, or the "ten words of Yahweh" as it is often expressed in the Jewish Bible. The first three commandments deal with man's proper relationship with his Creator and God; the other seven concern man's relationships with his fellow man.

Over the centuries Catholic theologians have developed lengthy and detailed treatises on morality based on the Ten Commandments. Up to the seventeenth century the moral teaching of the Church was treated as a part of general or doctrinal theology. In the 1600s there was a rapid development in the science of "moral theology". Accordingly, it gradually split off from dogmatic theology and tended to become a more or less independent science, with its roots, of course, in the doctrine of the Church.

After this short introduction to moral theology, I propose to take up each of the Ten Commandments. Some will be given more space than others. But in the context of the Ten Commandments we will try to present the solid and accepted moral teaching of the Church on most of the major areas of morality.

7

ADORE GOD, AND HIM ALONE

When the existence of the true God is denied or doubted, men tend to create their own gods, more to their liking. A convenient aspect of created gods is that they are much more manageable than the living God who created the heavens and the earth. We live in a time of widespread denial of God, for atheism, often disguised as a compassionate humanism, has become the "religion" of millions.

To be a real atheist, it is not necessary to tell everyone, "I am an atheist," and then proceed to offer some pseudo argument from science or from the problem of evil in order to "prove" that God does not exist.

Certainly, there are many among us who proceed in this fashion. Much more common, however, is the practice of atheism, that is, one lives *as if* there were no God, *as if* the soul were not immortal, *as if* there will be no final accountability to the Eternal Judge, *as if* there were no heaven or hell. Such foolish persons are actual or practical atheists, even though they may say that they believe in God. A notable characteristic of our time is the tremendous growth in the number of such practical atheists. Since man is born with an irresistible impulse to worship and seek God, if he denies God then he always sets up false gods and false idols.

The First Commandment of God gives the atheist something to think and worry about. In the first place God says, "I am the Lord your God. You shall not have strange gods before me." According to the traditional understanding of the Church, this Commandment positively prescribes the practice of the virtue of religion and negatively forbids everything that is contrary to religion.

Religion is concerned with man's relationship to his Creator and Lord. The virtue of religion is the moral virtue by which we are disposed to render to God the worship he deserves. It will be very helpful for us to consider some of the implications of the worship that we owe to God. "Worship" is the name that we give to the reverence we show almighty God. The word is also sometimes used in reference to veneration of the saints and the Blessed Virgin Mary, but without an overtone of "adoration" which is offered to God alone.

Worship of God is put into practice by adoration, prayer and sacrifice. We will say something now about adoration, leaving the other two notions for a later consideration.

Adoration usually suggests an image of someone bowing or kneeling or prostrate before God. These bodily postures, of course, were borrowed from the external honor that was shown to oriental kings and potentates in the past. When applied to God, they signify man's total dependence on God for everything that he is and has. Since God is the source of all reality, by adoring him we give expression to that knowledge and belief. True adoration for man involves both his body and his mind, that is, an exterior sign of reverence accompanied by a mental act of submission to God.

Only God may be adored, since he alone is the Supreme Being, source of all that is. Adoration is different from the veneration offered to Mary and to the saints. Often Protestants and other non-Catholics, seeing Catholics praying the Rosary or kneeling in prayer before a statue of a saint such as St. Francis or St. Theresa, accuse Catholics of offering adoration to the saints. Those who know their catechism know that this is a false accusation. We honor and venerate the saints because they are God's heroes. Whatever good deeds they accomplished on earth, and whatever sanctity they may have attained, was completely dependent on the grace of God.

Saints are saints because they responded heroically to the abundant graces God offered them. They are the heroes and the heroines of the faith. By dedicating churches in their honor, by honoring images of them, by praying to them, we are in reality acknowledging the wonders that God achieved in these weak human beings by the power of his grace. Every Catholic with a modicum of training in his faith knows that we do not adore statues or saints. That would be the abomination of idolatry, which is explicitly condemned by the First Commandment.

8

THE NEED FOR SACRIFICE

"I am the Lord your God. You shall not have strange gods before me." The First Commandment positively prescribes the worship of God and negatively forbids idolatry, superstition, sacrilege and anything that would dishonor our Creator and Lord. We might be tempted to think that the ancient peoples were crude in their worship of idols, that modern, scientific man does not do such things, and that therefore we do not have to worry about violations of the First Commandment because, since we have now "come of age", we are above such childish behavior.

Actually, we are creating small and large idols all the time. In a certain sense, every time we sin, every time we prefer a creature to the Creator, we are setting up "strange gods" and falling away from the true God.

We all know that adoration of God is one of the basics of our Catholic religion. In the last section we made a few observations about the nature of adoration. Now is the time to expand on that a little.

Adoration always involves some kind of recognition

of the absolute supremacy of God and of our total dependence on him. One of the most fundamental types of adoration is "sacrifice"—an idea that is often misunderstood and in any event is not popular in today's pleasure-seeking world.

Often when we pray to God we proclaim our love and devotion for him. But St. Ignatius Loyola said in his *Spiritual Exercises* that love is shown more in deeds than in words. A true sacrifice is shown in deeds more than in words. The requirements of a valid sacrifice are that some object, normally a desirable or valuable object, is offered to God as a sign of man's total dependence on him and of his subjection to the Lord. There is such a thing as a sacrificial mentality—a readiness to give up something for the love of God. But a real sacrifice requires more than that, in order to make it clear that the offerer is sincere. It requires that the object is actually surrendered to God, destroyed, or completely removed from the possession or control of the one making the sacrifice.

In this sense, the supreme sacrifice for a human being is to offer up his life for another. As our Lord said, "Greater love than this no man has, that a man lay down his life for a friend." And that is exactly what Jesus himself did for us on Calvary—he offered up his life to his Father as a propitiation for our sins. He took our sins upon himself and suffered in our place, he, the perfectly innocent One.

The Mass is a re-presentation now, in an unbloody manner, of the bloody sacrifice of the Cross over nineteen hundred years ago. Since it is a re-offering of Jesus on Calvary, the Mass is rightly referred to as "the holy

Sacrifice of the Mass", although we do not hear this expression much today. It has been replaced by the more general and vague "liturgy", which also applies to the celebration of the other sacraments.

Every dimension of human existence can, and often does, require sacrifices. There are certain things that we have to give up, that are taken away from us, and so forth. But a sacrifice to God, a religious sacrifice, is one that is *freely given* to God as a sign of reverence and submission to him. Such sacrifices are very meritorious in the sight of God, because they are basically acts of love of God and that is what God wants from us more than anything else—love. Love must be free; it cannot be forced and it cannot be bought.

Catholics should get into the habit of making small sacrifices for God. Sacrifices come in thousands of different forms: fasting, penances of various kinds, controlling vain curiosity to see and hear everything, giving up smoking or drinking during Lent, getting up early to attend a weekday parish Mass, denying oneself sweet desserts on occasion, and so on. If you are familiar with the life of any saint, male or female, young or old, you will know what I am talking about. For there has never been a saint who did not practice some kind of sacrificial self-denial.

Our Lord said, if you want to be my followers you must take up your cross daily and follow me. Those who try to lead a Christian life cannot expect to avoid what Jesus did not avoid—the Cross. As many Christian writers have pointed out in the past, the baffling thing about the Cross is that we all have to carry it—whether we want to or not. For those who accept it and submit to God, it is salvific; for those who reject it, it is the occasion of damnation. We should often pray for the grace to be able to accept and offer up the crosses that the Lord sends us.

9

WATCH AND PRAY

In addition to adoration and sacrifice, the worship of God mandated by the First Commandment is also carried out by personal prayer. In the Bible there are hundreds of references to prayer. Abraham prayed, Moses prayed, David prayed. The incomparable Psalms of the Old Testament are one hundred and fifty prayers of great variety and incredible beauty.

When we read the Gospels we see that Jesus prayed often—frequently spending the whole night in prayer. He prayed for forty days in the desert in preparation for his public ministry. It was during this time that the devil tempted him to abandon his mission of saving the human race. By prayer and fasting Jesus overcame the devil.

Jesus set a good example, but he also urged his disciples to pray. "Watch and pray, that you may not enter into temptation. The spirit indeed is willing, but the flesh is weak" (Mt 26:41). St. Paul wrote to his converts: "Pray without ceasing. In all things give thanks; for this is the will of God in Christ Jesus regarding you all" (1 Th 5:16–18). And St. James said: "The unceasing prayer of a just man is of great avail" (5:16).

So the lesson from Holy Scripture is clear: we should be constant in prayer. That, of course, is easier said than done. Many people find prayer difficult, either because they think they do not know how to pray or because they are so distracted by their interests and anxieties that they cannot concentrate on what they are doing.

Actually, prayer is quite simple. It is similar to our dealings with our loved ones. When we are with them we are aware of their presence, we talk to them, we ask them for favors. Our heavenly Father is always with us. He is aware of our distress; he knows what we need even before we ask him for anything. He will grant our requests if we ask him, but he does want us to ask.

An essential aspect of prayer is awareness of the presence of God within us and around us. When we pray we try to bring into our consciousness the creature-Creator relationship and all that that implies. To some, that will suggest asking God for favors; to others it will suggest thanking God for favors received; to still others it will lead to acts of adoration or sorrow for sin.

The division of prayer into two kinds, mental and vocal, is well known. The idea of "mental prayer" seems to frighten many people. Apparently, it conjures up for them an image of some saint in an ecstasy or the mystical prayer of a St. John of the Cross. Mental prayer is really not all that complicated, since it merely means to think about God and react to those thoughts with sentiments of faith, hope and charity. One of the best ways to begin praying mentally is to take a few lines from one of the Gospels, read them over carefully a few times, and then begin to reflect on their meaning—both in the situation to which they refer and in their relevance to me here and now. Thinking about God and loving him in return—that is the heart of mental prayer. Many people pray that way often without knowing that they are doing it. The mother busy in the home or the father driving to work often engage in mental prayer.

All prayer involves talking to God in one way or another. In the course of mental prayer we talk to God in our own words. What distinguishes vocal prayer from mental prayer is that, in speaking to God, we use the words of another. This is obvious when we pray the Our Father, Hail Mary, Memorare, Hail Holy Queen, and so forth. Both kinds of prayer, however, require mental attention to what we are doing. The Rosary is a marvelous combination of both types of prayer, since we think about the mysteries of salvation while we recite our familiar prayers.

"Watch and pray, that you may not enter into temptation." Our Lord gave that good advice to his Apostles both by example and by exhortation. It is advice that we should take to heart.

The Ten Commandments are not just a list of "don'ts". They also give us much positive direction on what we must do in order to be saved. Prayer is absolutely essential for salvation. When we pray we are offering God a form of worship that is very pleasing to him. And we are thereby living out God's First Commandment in a positive way.

10

SUPERSTITION WEARS MANY FACES

By his First Commandment God our Creator binds us to show him honor by acts of adoration, sacrifice and prayer. By failing to honor God by such acts we can be guilty of sins against the first law of God. Such sins would, of course, be sins of *omission*. There are also sins of *commission* against the First Commandment. The first group of these sins, which we will consider now, is offered under the general notion of "superstition".

We should not think that, since we live in a scientific, technological age, superstition is not in our midst, that it is a sin confined to primitive peoples—either those living today or those who lived in ancient biblical times. Not at all. Superstition is a human failing that has plagued man from the beginning of recorded history.

Superstition is an act of reverence or honor towards God that is false or superfluous. It comes in many different forms. It would be superstitious, for example, for a Catholic to offer worship to God according to Hindu or Buddhist rituals. It is also superstitious to expect God to grant favors for a definite number of prayers offered, for praying in a certain position or at a certain time. Accordingly, the Church periodically warns the faithful not to get involved in such practices as "chain prayers"—since the assumption underlying such prayers is that God is somehow forced to answer them in a way that man desires.

Superstition is the attempt to obtain special effects or knowledge beyond the powers of nature by invoking or using a creature as though it were divine or had divine powers. There are many types of such superstition, but the most common are divination, magic, sorcery and satanism.

Divination is the attempt to acquire knowledge that belongs to God alone by resorting to occult methods. Popular forms of divination are crystal gazing, reading tea leaves, palm reading, the horoscope, spiritism and seances. The popularity of these and other forms of the occult can be easily confirmed by checking the shelves of any modern bookstore. Large sums of money are involved in the promotion of the occult.

In our society *magic* now usually refers to sleight-of-hand tricks performed for the sake of entertainment. As such, it is a useful skill and has no reference to superstition. However, there are forms of "magic" that resort to preternatural powers and communication with the devil. Magic in this sense dishonors God and is a serious sin against the First Commandment.

Sorcery and *witchcraft* are practices that claim preternatural knowledge and attempt to produce marvelous effects. Often the devil is involved, either directly or indirectly, in these superstitions. Those who engage in them sometimes are possessed by the devil. The Church does not abandon such unfortunate persons, however, since she provides the rite of exorcism under certain conditions.

A sign of the growing atheism and godlessness of our time is the recent rise of the practice of "devil worship" or *Satanism* among Americans. There are even legally established and recognized "churches of Satan" where the enemy of God and of mankind is explicitly and deliberately invoked in opposition to and independently of God our Creator. Devil worship of all kinds is a mortal sin, since it attributes divine powers to Satan, himself a creature, and affirms that the same devil can function in the world independently of God.

Above, I have enumerated a few of the many forms of popular superstition. There are many more, such as fear of black cats, avoiding the number thirteen, trust in horoscopes (a multi-million dollar business), faith in a rabbit's foot, fear of walking under a ladder, and so forth. Catholic Christians should not be dominated by such vain and stupid superstitions. Our Lord Jesus Christ has freed us, through grace, from all such pagan nonsense.

The much-maligned *Baltimore Catechism* (no. 3) provides good direction in this matter: "Superstition is by its nature a mortal sin, but it may be venial either when the matter is slight or when there is a lack of full consent to the act. Often this sin is not mortal when there is question of certain popular superstitions, for example, belief in unlucky days and numbers, or when superstitious acts are performed as a joke without any serious thought of attributing divine powers to a creature, or when these acts are performed for amusement" (no. 212). And let us heed the words of Deuteronomy (18:10–12):

> There must never be anyone among you who makes his son or daughter pass through fire, who practices divination, who is soothsayer, augur or sorcerer, who uses charms, consults ghosts or spirits, or calls up the dead. For the man who does these things is detestable to the Lord, your God. . . .

Children are often attracted by the occult and are easily deceived. Parents should warn their children to avoid all superstitions and should tell them clearly why they are sinful. As a practical conclusion, superstitious games or instruments such as tarot cards, Ouija boards and the like should never be given to children as Christmas presents and should never be allowed into a Catholic home.

11

MODERN IDOLATORS

"I am the Lord your God. You shall not have strange gods before me" (Ex 20:2–3). We have been considering some of the implications of this First Commandment—both what it commands and what it prohibits. We have considered superstition and saw that it means giving false worship to God or divine honors to a creature. This latter notion is called "idolatry".

Idolatry in the strict sense means the worship of some image or "idol". Such idols are usually artistic representations of creatures which are believed to have superhuman powers. The idols can be representations of outstanding men, such as the Caesars of the Roman Empire, or images of various animals, birds, reptiles. Before the advent of Christ, such idol worship was common in the ancient world. Christianity was quite successful in rooting out idolatry, so much so that it has been of rare occurrence in the Western world for many centuries.

The purpose of idolatry is to show divine honors to a creature which is thought to be a supreme being of some kind. As such it is an act of religion—though false religion. Idolatry can proceed from ignorance, as when the idolators do not know the true God and so select some powerful creature, such as the sun or the moon, as the object of their reverence. As in all worship, the purpose is to appease the god, to ward off dangers and to ask for blessings of various kinds. Idolatry was an abomination to the Israelites of the Old Testament. The sacred authors delighted in heaping scorn on the idols of the pagans among whom they lived. Thus we read in Psalm 115: "their idols, in silver and gold, products of human skill, have mouths, but never speak, eyes, but never see, ears, but never hear . . . and not a sound from their throats."

Since idolatry involves a denial of the sovereignty of God over his creation, it is a direct violation of the First Commandment and is an offense against the virtue of religion. It is also opposed to the theological virtues of charity and faith, because it does not render to God the adoration which is his due and it involves a denial of the truth that faith professes.

Are modern, technological Americans prone to idol worship? The answer to that question, it seems to me, depends on how you understand the word "idol". Idol worship in the strict sense of setting up images of bulls or snakes for divine worship is almost non-existent in this country. However, there are many other forms of idolatry that men and women can fall into. If we understand by "idol" any creature that is regarded by a human being as the supreme being or absolute of his whole existence, then we immediately move into the area of idolatry, though now in a figurative sense.

Modern, secularized, technical man is attempting to create a world without God. In the thinking of millions of people, science, evolution and progress provide a sufficient explanation for the origin of life and man. A sense of self-sufficiency has led to a wholesale rejection of God in formerly Christian countries such as the United States. For some people atheism is a creed to be professed. Millions of others, however, though claiming with their lips to believe in God, actually live as if there were no God. They are what I like to call "practical atheists".

Nature cannot tolerate a vacuum. The same is true in the mind of man. With the whole weight of his nature, man, whether he consciously recognizes it or not, seeks the living God. Modern man, no matter how free or independent, must have some absolute outside of himself on which he can depend. Thus, he will either have the true God, who is there, or, if he rejects God, he will create a supreme being for himself—a god who is not there.

The number of possible objects for adoration, in place of the God who is, is not many. Some choose to worship themselves or some other individual. Thus, we now often hear such expressions as "I adore you." In the realm of creatures there are a few that give the appearance of being infinite, so they are better suited to be made into idols for worship. The most common are: money, power, fame or glory, scholarship, sexual pleasure and, on the lowest scale, food and drink. If a person's whole life is dedicated to the pursuit of one of these, or a combination of them, to the total neglect of God almighty, then that person is guilty of idolatry. He or she is giving divine honors to a creature, instead of worshiping the Creator of all things.

12

TREAT HOLY THINGS
IN A HOLY MANNER

One can sin against the First Commandment either by offering God a false worship, such as idolatry or superstition, or by failing or refusing to worship God as he should be worshiped. Let us consider two sins that come under this latter heading. The first is *tempting God*.

In everyday conversation it is not unusual to hear someone say, "That would be tempting God." What does the expression mean?

Obviously, it does not mean trying to incite God to evil—which would be sheer nonsense. The expression "tempting God" is perhaps clearer if we say instead "testing God". Testing God means that a person says or does something as an experiment to find out if God is all-powerful, provident, or has some other divine attribute.

A sin of this kind is explicit if someone challenges God to work a miracle in order to prove that he is all-good. This happens at times when someone, critically ill from cancer or as the result of an automobile accident, "tests" the power and goodness of God by demanding that he work a miracle in order to show his concern.

Another form of testing God is present when an individual recklessly exposes his life to danger, while thinking that, since God is so good, he will protect him from harm. The Lord expects us to use our intelligence, since that is why he gave it to us, and to take the normal precautions to safeguard our life.

God can and does work miracles, but only according to his inscrutable will, and not because a person demands a miracle.

A second defect in proper worship of God is a *sacrilege*. A sacrilege is the violation or irreverent treatment of a person, place or thing publicly dedicated to the worship or service of God. Of its very nature, sacrilege is a grievous sin, but it may be venial either because the matter is slight or because there is lack of full consent.

A sacrilege is *personal* when the act is directed against a person in Holy Orders or a religious who has vowed his or her life to God, for example, mugging a priest or raping a nun. It is *local* when a crime is committed in a holy place, such as a church. Thus robbery or murder in a church is a local sacrilege.

A sacrilege is *real* when a sacred object, such as the Blessed Sacrament or a chalice or a monstrance or holy water, is treated with contempt. Anyone who receives the Blessed Eucharist, while in the state of mortal sin, commits this type of sacrilege. Our people, especially our young people, must be reminded of this serious offense against the holiness of God, since we live in a time when confessions have declined drastically, while communions are up considerably.

The First Commandment reminds us of the holiness of God. The Israelites of Old Testament times had great awe of and reverence for the majesty of the Lord. Living in a time of increasing secularism (godlessness) and secularization (removal of God from public life and public consciousness), Catholics should often be reminded of the importance of the sacred in their holy religion. They should also be urged, especially on the occasion of great feasts like Christmas, "to treat holy things in a holy manner" (*sancta sancte tractanda*). This is and has been a primary concern of the holy Catholic Church since the very beginning.

13

SIMON THE MAGICIAN

In the eighth chapter of the Acts of the Apostles St. Luke recounts the story of Simon the Magician. According to Luke, Simon had developed quite a following because of his skill in performing tricks. Then Philip came along, preached the Gospel to the town and converted a number of people, including Simon. When Peter and John came to town some marvelous things accompanied the laying on of hands. Simon, being somewhat of a showman, desired to have the same power that the Apostles had and so he offered money to them in exchange for the power to communicate the Holy Spirit through the imposition of hands. Peter denounced the wretch and threatened him with divine wrath. Whereupon the poor Simon repented of his sin of trying to buy a spiritual gift.

We may piously hope that Simon saved his soul, but since apostolic times his name has been attached to the sin of buying and selling spiritual things. This particular sin against the First Commandment is called "simony". It is most commonly defined in the words of St. Thomas

Aquinas: "A deliberate design of selling or buying something spiritual or annexed to the spiritual."

At various times in the history of the Church simony was an all too common practice. Many are familiar with the scandal given around the time of the Reformation in the sixteenth century when indulgences were sometimes bought and sold. But over a thousand years before that, in the century that followed the edict of Constantine in 313 A.D., simony was practiced in the buying and selling of ecclesiastical offices, especially the priesthood and bishoprics. Thus, the Council of Chalcedon in 451 forbade the buying and selling of ecclesiastical offices. The reason for the traffic in Church offices was that often either great power or wealth or both were attached to them.

The Church has always been aware of the danger of simony and so she has, over the centuries, levelled severe penalties, including excommunication, on those who practice it.

What are some of the ways in which simony appears? It is simoniacal to sell any spiritual gift, such as a Church office, a sacrament, jurisdiction, indulgence. Simony is especially a danger in a country where there is a union between the Church and the state. When the two are separated, such as is the case in the United States, simony does not seem to be very common.

Is it simony to sell blessed chalices, stations of the cross, rosaries, and such like sacred objects? Here a distinction must be made. The objects may legitimately be sold at face value, depending on the worth of the material (gold or silver) or the artistry involved. But it would be simony to charge more than the material value because the object was used by a certain saint, or by a favorite pope, or because some indulgence is attached to the use of the object. It is also a sin of simony to sell relics of saints, although gold and silver *containers* for the relics, called "reliquaries", may be sold for the gold and silver they contain. In all of this the thing to watch out for is the buying and selling of *spiritual* goods. Blessed articles, such as rosaries, lose their blessing when they are sold and should be blessed again for regular use.

Sometimes Catholics are accused of simony because they offer priests money to celebrate Masses, or on the occasion of a wedding or funeral. Are such stipends simony? Although it may *appear* that Masses are being sold, actually the money is given to the priest for his upkeep and for the support of the Church. Since Vatican II there is a great variety in the way that stipends are handled: sometimes all of them go to the Church; sometimes the priest is allowed to keep the stipends offered to him; sometimes they are divided up in various ways.

There are priests now who receive regular salaries, as teachers, for example, and refuse to accept stipends. However, many priests and missionaries support themselves wholly or in great part by the stipends they receive, so that they would not be able to carry on their work without them.

The Lord gives his gifts freely—and so should the Church. Jesus had a special concern for the poor and destitute—and so should the Church. This means that the priest may never refuse his spiritual ministry just because the recipient is not able to offer him some money. The priest should freely give what he has freely received. However, the priest is a man; he has to live; he has dedicated his life to the service of the People of God. So it is their responsibility to support him. Conscious of this relationship, our Catholic people have always been most generous in their support of priests and religious.

14

BLESSED BE
THE NAME OF THE LORD FOREVER

One clear sign of the growing paganization of American society is the dramatic increase in the irreverent use of the holy name of God. What strikes me especially is the filth and profanity that I so often hear coming from the lips of children. If it is true that "out of the abundance of the heart the mouth speaks" (cf. Mt 12:34), then the widespread irreverence in the use of the holy name of God would seem to be one more indication of the increasing atheism and godlessness in our country.

The children, however, are not the only ones to blame. Children imitate their parents and the adults they come in contact with. If parents take the name of God in vain, then is it any wonder that their children do the same? And what about the media? There is no need to recount here how the names of God and of Jesus are taken in vain, especially in the printed word, on certain television programs and in many films.

The Bible threatens dire punishments on those who misuse the sacred name of the Lord (Yahweh). Thus we read in Exodus (20:7) the Second Commandment of God: "You shall not utter the name of Yahweh your God to misuse it, for Yahweh will not leave unpunished the man who utters his name to misuse it" (*Jerusalem Bible*).

With Shakespeare, we might ask "What is in a name?" The ancient Israelites of the Old Testament did not make a clear distinction, as we do, between the name of God and God himself. The very name of "Yahweh" was thought to contain God himself. Therefore the name was to be treated with the same respect that one would show to God himself. Literally this is not quite accurate, but there is much to be said for the idea, since names of persons stand for those persons. Just consider the important role of personal signatures in our society. Without personal signatures the whole world of banking, and perhaps most of the bureaucracy of our technological society, could not function. For, a signature on a check for one thousand dollars (merely a piece of paper) is a guarantee that the signer will pay one thousand dollars to the addressee of the check. So, in a very true sense, the signature (name) of a person stands for that person.

By the Second Commandment we are directed always to speak with reverence of God, of Mary, of the Saints and of holy things. When the holy name of God is invoked, it should be either in prayer or in an attitude of reverence for our Lord and creator. Our lips and tongue betray what we are. If we have interior reverence and respect for God and all things holy, then we will be most careful in speaking about them. On the other hand, if we habitually disregard God's law, if we rarely think of God or if we resent God's creative authority over us, then this will manifest itself by means of the words that cross our lips. Thus, it is truly distressing to God-fearing Catholics to have to associate with persons who constantly take the name of the Lord in vain by saying, "O God," or "O Jesus," or "Jesus Christ" in order to express some suprise or to give emphasis to a statement. Such utterances are instances of taking God's name in vain, and in most cases are probably venial sins. Parents should set a good example for their children by avoiding such profanity; they should also not tolerate the misuse of God's holy name by their children. When I was a boy, children would get their mouths washed out with soap for taking God's name in vain. Such a remedy may not be a certain cure, but it surely got the point across.

What is in a name? For one thing, eternal salvation. The Old Testament tells us repeatedly that the holy name of God is to be praised, that the Lord will save those who call upon him for assistance. There is great power in the name of "Jesus Christ", since "Jesus" means "savior", and "Christ" means "messiah" or "the anointed one of the Lord". Stressing the power inherent in the name of Jesus, St. Peter told the Jewish leaders in Jerusalem, according to St. Luke's account in Acts (4:12): "For of all the names in the world given to men, this is the only one by which we can be saved."

Perhaps the Second Commandment is one that we do not often advert to. But the sincere Christian is one who has great reverence for God and for his holy name. In this age of increasing vulgarity, profanity, atheism and ridicule of God and his saints we Catholics should be especially careful, not only from a desire of worship of God but also in order to make reparation to him, always to use God's holy name with great reverence and reserve. Let ours be the sentiment of the psalmist in Psalm 112 (2–3): "Blessed be the name of the Lord both now and forever. From the rising to the setting of the sun is the name of the Lord to be praised."

15

SWEARING AND PERJURY

The Second Commandment forbids the misuse of God's holy name. It also requires that his name be used reverently. One of the ways in which God's name may be used reverently is by swearing or by taking an oath.

An oath as defined by moral theologians is an invocation of God as a witness to the truth of an assertion or to the sincerity of a promise.

Although some Protestants reject all oaths, Jesus did not forbid them and rules for oaths are given in the Old Testament. Jesus himself took an oath before the Jewish Council. But his will is that we should normally deal with each other without having to confirm what we say by oaths. Jesus said: "I say to you not to swear at all . . . let your speech be 'Yes, yes'; 'No, no'; and whatever is beyond these comes from the evil one" (cf. Mt 5:34–37).

However, at times and for very serious reasons, it is necessary to give special force to what a person says by calling upon God to witness to the truth of a statement. Thus, our law courts require witnesses to take an oath in support of the truth of their assertions. Deliberately to tell a lie while under such an oath is the sin of perjury. Perjury is a mortal sin since it blasphemes God who knows all things and is all holy; it also destroys the faith and trust that are necessary among men in order to establish human community. It is a sin to swear an oath without sufficient reason or without being absolutely sure of the truth to which one swears.

If a person has to make a solemn promise about some important matter he may call upon God to witness to the fact that he intends to keep his promise. This type of oath is called an "oath of promise". As in the case of assertory oaths, promissory oaths must not be taken without sufficient reason and they may concern only good objects. Oaths of this kind are common: for example, many marriage formulae call upon God to witness to the promise of love and fidelity. Government officials in certain positions, such as the president, justices of the Supreme Court, commissioned officers in the armed forces and so forth, must swear a promissory oath to defend the Constitution of the United States. Those who take such oaths have a serious obligation before God to carry out what they have promised to the best of their ability. When a Catholic Christian takes such an oath, it is always understood that the oath does not include the observance of any law that goes contrary to the law of God or the law of the Church.

Thus a Catholic is not bound by any law that would require him or her to approve abortion, euthanasia, sterilization, discrimination, falsehood and so forth.

Today there is such looseness in the use of language that many words related to oaths are used incorrectly. Thus, "swearing" is not necessarily wrong. In fact, it can be good and holy. The Second Commandment forbids the use of illicit oaths. "Cursing" means to call down evil on another. "Perjury" means to invoke God as a witness to a deliberate lie.

Catholics should be very careful in the use of God's holy name. The names of God, Jesus, Mary and the names of the saints should be used only in a reverent way. This usually means in the context of prayer or in speaking about those things that pertain to God.

As a general rule, oaths should be studiously avoided, since they are not needed in relations between believers. When they are required, either in civil or ecclesiastical courts, then the one who takes the oath should know exactly what he or she is doing.

All should be alerted to the very serious nature of perjury. Public officials and those who appear regularly in courts of law should take great care to avoid perjury of any kind. Human society simply cannot exist if there is no trust among individuals. It is for this reason that lying is wrong, since it tends to destroy human community. Perjury, however, not only offends against the neighbor by reason of the lie, but it also shows contempt for God since it calls upon God to be a witness to a lie. We were horrified at the perjury involved in the Watergate scandal. Let us see to it that we avoid all unnecessary oaths and that, if we must swear, we be most careful to speak the truth and nothing but the truth.

16

THE CATHOLIC VIEW OF VOWS

Many Catholics, and perhaps most of them, do not seem to be aware of the fact that vows made to God are governed by the Second Commandment. A vow is a deliberate promise made to God by which a person binds himself or herself under pain of sin to do something that is especially pleasing to God. Thus, since the holy name of God is invoked, in vows, they pertain to the Second Commandment.

In making a vow a person must act with freedom, knowledge and deliberation, and with the intention of binding himself under sin. What is promised by any vow must be possible for the one taking the vow. It must also be morally good; hence any vow to do something evil is not only invalid but is also sinful. Finally, a vow must be better than its contrary. Thus, it would be frivolous to vow to sit on the right side in church on Sunday rather than on the left side, since neither is better than the other.

Vows to God can cover a wide range of personal actions or things. We are most familiar with the three vows of nuns and male religious: poverty, chastity and obedience. A person may take a vow to say certain prayers each day, to attend a certain number of Masses, to make a pilgrimage to the Holy Land, to give money to a holy shrine, to build a chapel in honor of the Sacred Heart or of some saint, and so forth.

The Catholic Church distinguishes between different kinds of vows. A vow is said to be *public* if it is taken in the name of the Church and is accepted by some ecclesiastical superior; otherwise it is *private*. The vows of religious are public, while the vow of a lay person to make a pilgrimage to Jerusalem is a private vow. A vow is *personal* if it concerns the conduct of the one who takes it, e.g., a vow of perpetual chastity. A vow is said to be *real* if some physical object or thing is promised to God, such as a donation to the National Shrine in Washington, D.C.

Since a vow is a deliberate promise made to God, it binds under pain of sin, either mortal or venial, depending upon the matter vowed or the intention of the one who takes the vow. Generally speaking, if the matter vowed is serious, then the obligation is serious, such as in the vows of religious or in the vow of celibacy of diocesan priests. If the matter is slight, such as saying one "Our Father" each day, then the obligation would be slight.

Outside of the vows involved in the priestly and religious life, American Catholics have not been accustomed to taking vows. Here or there a person may take a vow to enter religious life or to practice perpetual virginity, but it does not seem to be in the religious makeup of most Americans to bind themselves to do good works by means of vows. There was a time in Europe when vows among the laity were quite common. Manuals on moral theology, which until just a few years ago were carefully studied by all candidates for the priesthood, contain detailed instructions for the future confessor on how to deal with those who take or want to take vows. Now one rarely hears the subject of vows discussed, unless it has to do with the dispensation of vows for nuns, religious and priests. A dispensation releases one from the obligation of a vow; it may be granted only by the competent religious superior for a just reason and in the name of God. Normally those who have jurisdiction over public vows are the Holy Father, the local Ordinary or Bishop, the Superiors and Superioresses of religious orders and congregations.

In recent years we have witnessed the sad spectacle of thousands of nuns and religious abandoning their religious vows. Some have just walked out, but most have been dispensed by their religious superiors. This infidelity on the part of so many religious, it seems to me, has had a deleterious effect on many married people and has weakened their resolve to remain faithful to their marriage vows. Personally, I have no doubt that there is an intimate connection between the defection of thousands of priests and religious and the very increased rate of divorce among Catholics.

Catholics are often asked to defend the legitimacy of vows. Protestants, it seems, for the most part do not believe in vows. In the Catholic view a vow to do some good deed makes that deed "better" or "more virtuous", since it unites the person to God by a new bond of the virtue of religion. So what is done is not only good in itself, it is also an act of worship of God. Those who take a vow deliberately surrender to God their moral freedom of acting otherwise. So taking a vow is an act of intense love of God. Vows also take direct aim at our all-pervasive human weakness since they do not leave matters of worship and salvation to caprice or feeling.

17

BLASPHEMY AND CURSING

We will conclude our reflections on the Second Commandment with a few words about blasphemy and cursing.

Blasphemy is any speech or gesture that manifests contempt for God. The blasphemer is one who, while believing in God and recognizing his holiness, deliberately insults him out of fear, anger, hatred, despair or some other deep human emotion. Blasphemy is one of the sins that Catholic moral theologians mention as a mortal sin by its very nature. There may be mitigating circumstances, such as uncontrollable rage, that would make the sin venial by reason of lack of due deliberation, but the sin of blasphemy of itself is a very serious offence against the goodness of God.

It is blasphemous, for example, to call God stupid, cruel or unjust, or to shake one's fist against heaven.

Blasphemy may be directed immediately against God himself, or only mediately, that is, when the Church, the Blessed Virgin Mary, the saints or sacred things are reviled.

Blasphemy was considered such a serious offense in the Old Testament that it was punished by stoning to death. It was the chief accusation made against Jesus by the leaders of Israel (cf. Mt 26:63–66).

It is difficult to say to what extent blasphemy, as a formal sin, is a sin into which Americans fall. Because of the almost universal presence of suffering and evil in human society and human history, there seems to be a strong tendency on the part of some to blame God for all of it—fires, wars, murders, sickness, treachery, and so forth. Since God is all-perfect and infinite goodness, he cannot directly will evil. Hence, the source of evil is the perverse use of the created will, but in times of stress many persons tend to forget that and want to blame God for whatever happens. It could be that the tendency to attribute evil directly to God is the main form of blasphemy in our day.

A peculiarity about blasphemy is this: one must be a believer and have a certain awareness of God before he can commit a sin of blasphemy. The true atheist, if such there be, can hardly show contempt for a God whose existence he stoutly denies. Hence, this sin seems to be more common among peoples with a deep faith than it is in secularized and permissive societies such as we find in the United States.

In Western Europe laws against blasphemy have been on the books since the sixteenth century—basically since the Reformation. Before that time blasphemy was outlawed by Church law and handled by ecclesiastical courts. Many of the American colonies had laws against blasphemy. In fact, it still remains on the statute books of states such as Massachusetts, Pennsylvania, New Jersey and Maryland. Gradually, however, it was considered more an offense against society than an offense against God.

Cursing is also a violation of the Second Commandment. To curse is to call down evil on someone or something. Although in the Old Testament we see a number of examples of the cursing of enemies—examples that often perplex us and are very difficult to understand,—in the New Testament the cursing of enemies is strictly forbidden. Jesus commanded his followers to love their enemies, to pray for them and to be reconciled with them. He taught us in the Our Father to pray: "Forgive us our trespasses as we forgive those who trespass against us." This puts us in a very dangerous situation. For, if the forgiveness we receive from the Father is conditioned by the forgiveness we show to others, then, if we wish to have our sins forgiven, we ought to show mercy and kindness to those who have offended us.

Catholic moralists distinguish between cursing things less than man and cursing persons. To curse anything less than man is more or less wrong, mainly because of the impatience involved. The overused expression "God damn" this or that has lost much of its original meaning, but its use is an offense against the Second Commandment and it should be sedulously avoided. To curse people by wishing them evil is wrong—especially if moral evil and eternal damnation are called down on them. Such an act is always seriously sinful if done with full deliberation.

Language, speech, articulated thought are magnificent gifts of God. Without speech man would be reduced to the level of the brute beasts; with it he can aspire to the company of the angels and of the Lord God himself. Let us strive, with God's grace, to avoid all blasphemies and curses and to use our tongues to praise and to bless.

18

CHRIST, THE RISING SUN OF JUSTICE

Because the universe, the earth and our whole life belong to God we must spend some time on a regular basis in worshiping him and giving him thanks. Nature itself requires this, as we see plainly manifested in the religious customs of most peoples and cultures.

However, God manifested his precise will in this matter to the Israelites in the Old Testament when he gave Moses his Third Commandment: "Remember to keep holy the Sabbath day" (Ex 20:8). To the early Israelites this meant that no work was to be done on the Sabbath or Saturday. By the time of Jesus there were synagogues, so then the people would gather there for prayer and instruction on the holy day. The early Christian Church changed the day of worship from Saturday, the last day of the week, to Sunday, the first day. The principal reasons given in the tradition of the Church for this change are that Jesus rose from the dead on Sunday and also sent down the Holy Spirit on his Church on this day. Another reason given by St. Justin Martyr is that God created the world on this day. Sunday reminds us of Baptism and the new creation which began with our Lord's Resurrection. Sunday is also called "the Lord's Day" (Latin: *Dominica*; see Rev 1:10).

Please note these beautiful words of St. Maxim of Turin:

> We hold the Lord's Day in reverence and celebrate it solemnly, because on that day our Savior, like the rising sun,

shone in the light of his glorious resurrection after conquering the darkness of hell; this day is called Sunday, because Christ, the rising Sun of Justice, fills it with light.

In the first centuries of the Church there were no laws enjoining attendance at Mass on Sundays under pain of sin. It was simply assumed that all Christians would be present at the eucharistic liturgy, if at all possible. There they would be nourished by the Word of God and by the Body and Blood of Christ.

As the centuries moved on, however, the faith of many grew cool. Thus, from the sixth to the thirteenth centuries Church laws in the matter became more explicit, culminating in legislation for the whole Church that Mass attendance is obligatory every Sunday and holy day for all Catholics who have reached their seventh birthday.

Rarely, in the contemporary Catholic Church, do we hear any reference to the six precepts or commandments of the Church. How many Catholics even know what they are? Certainly they have not been abrogated, though there have been some modifications, such as the rules of fast and abstinence. The very first precept of the Church is: to assist at Mass on all Sundays and holy days of obligation. The six precepts are still binding and are still taught, but it seems that they are now taught separately and not as a group.

Since Vatican II there is a great reluctance on the part of bishops, priests, theologians and teachers to talk about the duties or responsibilities of the faithful in terms of "obligations", "commandments" and "binding under pain of sin". These expressions are not used much in our day, but the reality they signify has not changed.

Thus all Catholics over seven years of age who have

sufficient use of reason are bound under pain of mortal sin to attend Mass on Sunday if at all possible. Naturally, physical or moral impossibility excuse one from this obligation.

The Church has never said that Catholics are not morally bound to attend Mass "if they don't feel like it," contrary to what many Catholic teachers say in our colleges, high schools, grade schools and C.C.D. classes. The idea is, and the normal attitude of the Catholic should be, that he or she freely wishes to attend Mass on Sundays and holy days out of a sense of grateful love for God. But man's serious obligation to worship God on the "Sabbath" is nowhere conditioned, either in the Bible or in the tradition of the Church, by the qualification "if you feel like it." If it were, then the Third Commandment should read: "Remember to keep holy the Sabbath day, if you feel like it." That type of commandment is really no commandment—and the thinking behind it is foreign to Holy Scripture.

Men and women are free—and faith in Jesus Christ and his Church is a free gift. But Church law is still in force. So all I am saying here is what the official Church has been teaching explicitly since the thirteenth century: Catholics have a serious obligation in conscience to attend Mass on Sundays and holy days. Religious teachers of all kinds have the corresponding obligation to communicate this truth to their students.

After a number of years of laxity in this matter it is encouraging to note that more and more bishops are beginning to insist, once again, on the faithful observance by all of the Third Commandment.

19

WHAT ABOUT THE SUNDAY REST?

Observance of the Third Commandment requires two things of the faithful, namely, assistance at Mass and abstinence from work. In this essay we will offer a few reflections on the meaning of the Sunday rest.

When God on Mount Sinai commanded that every seventh day should be kept holy, he said: "Six days you shall labor, and do all your work; but the seventh day is a sabbath to the Lord your God; in it you shall not do any work, you, or your son, or your daughter. . . ." (Ex 20:9–10). As is commonly known, Jewish tradition has always insisted on the sacredness of the Sabbath which meant, originally, to abstain from all work on that day. After the exile, attendance at synagogue services became very common.

In 321 A.D. the Emperor Constantine ordered that Sunday was to be observed by all as a day of worship and rest. Most legal codes of Christian nations since that time have included some laws concerning the Sunday rest. The thirteen colonies had such laws as do most, perhaps all, of the fifty States at the present time.

The Sunday rest is something that characterizes Christian civilization. One may say with considerable accuracy that the level of observance of Sunday—both with regard to worship and with regard to rest—is a fair measure of the intensity of Christian faith in any country. With each year, one might almost say with each month, we are witnessing the rapid dechristianization or paganization of American culture. Is it not also true that, at the same time, we are seeing more and more gross violations of the Sunday rest? To give just one example, more department stores and businesses of all kinds are staying open on Sunday—apparently to keep up with the competition.

I do not know to what extent Catholics are involved in this profanation from the point of view of management, but they can do something about it as customers: avoid all unnecessary shopping on Sunday.

By not working one day a week, on the Lord's day, the Christian bears witness to the fact that he truly believes in the promises of Jesus Christ. He shows that his ultimate trust is in God and not in material goods. He is saying in effect: I pass up the opportunity to earn more money on the Lord's day because I know that I am made for heaven; my nature and my eternal destiny infinitely surpass the things of this world. The pagans work on Sunday because they have no hope in eternal life—and perhaps because they do not know any better.

What does the Sunday rest mean for an American in the 1980s? That is a very difficult question to answer. The main purpose, of course, is so that all will have the time and opportunity to attend Mass, to hear the Word of God and to receive our Lord in the Blessed Sacrament. In other ways, too, Sunday should be dedicated to the Lord, at least in intention, if not by the actual practice of other good works. Some activities that are in conformity with the Sunday observance are: reading the Bible or the life of some saint; praying the Rosary; engaging in serious conversation on God and the things of the spirit, and so forth.

Sunday should be a day of joy and relaxation. It is the time for a family meal, for healthy recreation, for sport, for taking a stroll or for going for a Sunday drive. In these and similar activities we can both praise God for his goodness and refresh our bodies and minds after the week's work.

Since the time of Moses, abstinence from all unnecessary work has been an essential part of the Sunday observance. We have all heard that the Church forbids all "servile" work on Sunday. Formerly "servile work" was defined as hard physical labor; thus, digging ditches, plowing, splitting wood, and so forth were said to be "servile" and so were forbidden on Sunday except in cases of emergency or real necessity.

In the past twenty years so many exceptions have been placed on the meaning of servile work by moral theologians that it is just about impossible to lay down general rules. Thus, many men who spend the whole week behind a desk find real refreshment in working in their garden, mowing the lawn, washing their car. Although these activities require physical labor, they are not now considered to be "servile" in the situation of contemporary technological America.

It seems to me that what all should try to do is to observe the spirit of Sunday—worship and rest and joy. If some kind of work does not fit into that pattern, and is truly unnecessary, then it should be avoided. If anyone has a serious doubt about whether or not he or she is violating God's law of the Sunday rest, then that person should seek the advice of a priest.

20

THE CHURCH CALENDAR:
A PERPETUAL CATECHESIS

In recent years there have been numerous suggestions advanced about how to revise the yearly calendar. These proposals are of great concern to the Catholic Church, since the Church structures the days, weeks and months of each year in a very special way in order to commemorate the mysteries of salvation.

In order to reveal himself to mankind God had to make use of human words, otherwise he would not have been able to communicate with us. God not only spoke to us by means of his Word; he also performed mighty deeds in order to save his people. Thus, we read in the Bible how God called Abraham, summoned Moses, led the Hebrews through the desert, and so forth. But the Old Testament was a preparation for the coming of the Messiah. The fullness of God's revelation took place in the birth, life, death, Resurrection and glorification of his only Son, our Lord Jesus Christ. It is important to remember always that Christianity is a historical religion, in the sense that it derives from historical events that occurred at a definite place and at a certain time.

As citizens of the United States we commemorate each year the major historical events related to the founding of our country, for example, July 4, George Washington's Birthday, Lincoln's Birthday, and so forth. In our personal lives each year we commemorate our birthday, our wedding anniversary if we are married.

This is proper and very natural because of the time pattern we live in due to days, weeks and years.

Now in the life of the Church there is such a thing as "sacred time", that is, liturgical seasons, feasts and fasts that commemorate the mysteries of our salvation. These seasons and feasts are sometimes referred to as "sacramentals" because they stimulate the faith of the people and dispose them to a more generous service to God.

For hundreds of years the Roman Calendar was centered around the "Christmas cycle" and the "Easter cycle". But from the Middle Ages on, more and more saints' days were added to the calendar so that, quite often, even the regular Sunday Mass was replaced by the Mass of some martyr or doctor of the Church.

The Second Vatican Council decided to "tidy up" the calendar by highlighting the major mysteries of our redemption and playing down the role of the saints "so that the entire cycle of the mysteries of salvation may be suitably recalled" (*Constitution on Sacred Liturgy*, 102).

Thus, there are now five major liturgical seasons in the course of each Church year. The one-year cycle begins with the first Sunday of Advent—usually the last Sunday in November. In Advent the coming of the Lord is anticipated—his first coming in Bethlehem, his coming to each person at death and his final or Second Coming at the end of the world.

In the Christmas season the earthly birth of Jesus is remembered, his infancy and childhood at Nazareth. Lent concentrates on the suffering and death of Jesus and on our need for penance and self-denial.

The Easter season recalls the Resurrection and Ascension of Jesus; it concludes with the commemoration of Pentecost—the descent of the Holy Spirit on the Apostles. The series of weeks from Pentecost to Advent, about twenty-eight weeks, has salvation history as its theme. It stresses God's loving concern for his Church and his call for a loving response from us. Then the cycle begins again.

In addition to the seasons there are the feasts of the saints, who are God's heroes and heroines. They are the men and women who have fully responded to the call of God's grace. So the Church sets them before us for our veneration and imitation. When the ecclesiastical calendar was revised in the 1960s about forty feasts of saints were eliminated, almost a hundred were made optional, and approximately sixty remained for general observance in the Roman Rite.

The feasts of the Blessed Virgin Mary, of course, are given a special place, as are those of St. Joseph, St. John the Baptist, and the Apostles, especially Sts. Peter and Paul.

As believing Catholics, the yearly Church calendar should be an important part of our daily lives. We should always know, for example, on any given Sunday or in any week, in which liturgical season we are. This is important relative to certain religious duties, such as receiving Holy Communion during the Easter season (Ash Wednesday to Trinity Sunday) or observing the proper fasts and abstinence.

Faithful adherence to the Church calendar is, in itself, a type of perpetual catechesis. For, by adverting to the seasons of the year we are reminded of God's gracious gifts to us. We are also summoned, by his Word and by his grace, to respond to his advances with generous acts of loving service.

21

FAST AND ABSTINENCE FOR CATHOLICS

Penance and self-denial should be an essential part of the life of every Christian. The basic idea behind penance is that we deprive ourselves of some good, such as food, drink, various kinds of pleasure, possessions, in order to break our natural attachments to such things and elevate our minds and hearts to the love of God.

Man is a unity of spirit and matter. The Lord is constantly summoning us to conversion—to turn away from creatures and selfishness and to turn to him. The first words that Jesus utters in the opening lines of St. Mark's Gospel are a call to penance, conversion and faith. But it is not enough merely to turn the mind to God and to make an act of faith. Faith must express itself in *deeds*; it must be externalized precisely because man is a complex reality of both spirit and matter. Also, mind and body reinforce each other, that is, faith and love lead to external acts and those external acts help to increase both faith and love.

In both Scripture and the tradition of the Church we find that fasting and abstinence are highly recommended as one good way to do penance. There are others of course, such as accepting the daily sufferings that God sends to each person, but fast and abstinence have a special place of honor because of the example of the prophets, of Jesus, of the saints and serious Christians of all ages. The Law of the Israelites commanded fasts at certain times. Jesus set an example for all time, since he began his public ministry with a fast of forty days in the wilderness near Jericho and the Jordan River. The Apostles fasted (Acts 13:2; 2 Cor 11:27); and in the early Church weekly fast days were soon observed, Wednesday and Friday being mentioned already in the first century.

In both East and West fast and abstinence have been observed at different times and in different ways. But by the Middle Ages the forty days' fast of Lent was well established in the West. In the 1950s Pope Pius XII introduced some changes with regard to the eucharistic fast from midnight. In 1964 and 1966 Pope Paul VI instituted further changes in the eucharistic fast and the whole spectrum of fast and abstinence in the Roman Catholic Church. It was his apostolic constitution *Paenitemini* in 1966 which established the Church practice that we are now living under. In that document the Holy Father explained how penance belongs to the heart of the Catholic faith. He also pointed out that different times call for different forms of penance; then he outlined how penance should be practiced in our day.

There is no doubt that the new norms are much easier than the old ones. Those who are over forty will recall how difficult it was to fast on all the weekdays in Lent, on the Ember Days four times a year, and on the vigils of the big feasts such as Christmas, the Assumption and the Immaculate Conception. The present thinking in the Church is that there should be more penance now than there was in the past, but that it should not be prescribed by law under pain of sin. Whether Catholics now are more penitential than formerly is hard to say. If one were to judge by externals, it would seem that fasting and abstaining are less common now that it is left to the conscience of each individual.

What do we mean by "fast" and "abstinence"? A fast day is one on which only one full meal is allowed; the other two meals should be cut down so that, taken together, they do not equal one full meal. Fasting in the current law of the Church binds those between the ages of 21 and 59; those who have reached the age of 14 are bound by abstinence. A day of abstinence is a day on which we are not allowed to eat any meat.

Fasting and abstinence are especially encouraged in Lent, but at present Church law does not require very much of us in this regard. In the United States all Fridays of Lent are now days of abstinence. Ash Wednesday and Good Friday are days of fast and abstinence—the only two such days now left in the Church calendar. Bishops may, for good reasons, dispense their people from fast and abstinence; they can also designate other days of fast or abstinence or both.

Many Catholics lament the passing of "fish on Friday" and the forty days' fast during Lent, even many of those who frequently violated the law. It was difficult, they say, but it helped to give the Catholic a sense of identity and a sense of belonging to a Christian community that was serious about its obligations to God. In addition to being penitential it was also highly symbolic. And symbols are extremely important in religion. We must do penance; if we do not, we will perish. Even though the Church does not now demand fasting during the week, I would like to recommend to all my readers that they fast one or two days during Lent, say, Wednesdays and Fridays. Also, it is a time-honored practice to give the money thus saved to the poor.

22

HONOR YOUR FATHER
AND YOUR MOTHER

Each of the Ten Commandments covers a special area of human concern. Each Commandment also presents certain difficulties of observance. Today perhaps more than ever before, because of the anti-authority current in modern society, the Fourth Commandment takes on vital importance. The Commandment itself, as proclaimed by Moses, says: "Honor your father and your mother, that your days may be long in the land which the Lord your God gives you" (Ex 20:12).

God therefore commands that we "honor" our natural parents. The divine command merely reaffirms what the natural law requires, since it is obvious that none of us would ever reach maturity if it were not for our parents, or someone else who takes their place, who brought us into the world and cared for us until we were old enough to provide for ourselves.

Man is by his very nature a social being. This means that he cannot either come into existence or develop into a mature person without the help and cooperation of other human beings. Associations of human beings are called "communities". By his birth the child is inserted into a number of different communities, the principal ones being the family, the state and the Church. Communities can function only if there is some authority that directs the members, in one way or another, to the stated or accepted goals of the community. Authority is here taken to mean the moral power or right to direct others to some end.

Since the family, therefore, is a community it follows that it possesses some authority. And since the family comes from God, the authority that resides in it also comes from God. That authority is located in the father and the mother. So God tells us through Moses to honor our father and mother. The "honor" due to parents has been understood in the Church for centuries to mean that we should love, reverence and obey our parents.

We love our parents by wishing them well, spending some time with them, praying for them and helping them in any way we can. We reverence our parents by speaking and acting towards them in a kindly manner, by seeking their advice as occasion warrants, by readily accepting their corrections and by patiently putting up with their faults.

Children should obey the lawful commands of their parents as long as they live under parental authority. In fact, children can sin grievously by disobeying the strict command of a parent in an important matter. However, children who do not live any longer under parental authority are not bound to follow the directions of their parents, though it is often good advice to at least listen to what they have to say. But even adult children are subject to parental authority in certain areas of everyday living, such as times for meals, coming home at night, etc., as long as they live under their parents' roof.

Many parents have a difficult time of it today in getting their children to obey them. There are many reasons for this. We live in an age that glorifies personal freedom, sometimes to the point of license, at the expense of authority. Children are frequently urged

—by the media, by their peers and sometimes even by their teachers in school—to challenge and resist parental authority. This gives rise to serious conflicts in many families. It seems to me that early and frequent schooling of children in the divine command of obedience to one's parents would help to improve this situation. Also, parents must insist on and require reasonable obedience from their children from the earliest age.

There is not much that concerned parents can do about the anti-authority current in our culture, but they should discuss the problem openly with their children when they reach the age at which they can understand the state of the question. But I think that parents should personally challenge any teacher of their children who tries to turn their children against them in disobedience. Such teachers should be immediately confronted.

A very serious problem now related to the Fourth Commandment is the care of mother and father in their old age. Some "rest homes" are good, but many are a scandal. No general rule can be laid down in this matter, but children who place their parents in one of these homes should see to it that they are not using the home as a way of avoiding their duties to their parents. The obligation to obey parents ceases at some point, but the obligation to love and reverence them never ceases. If a parent is placed in such a home it must be done for the right reason and after all other possibilities have been explored.

23

LOVE FOR ONE'S RELATIVES

In the Fourth Commandment God tells us to show reverence, love and obedience towards our parents. Under this Commandment are included our relations to the members of our family and also our relations to other authorities, such as employers, the state and the Church. Let us reflect on the implications of some of these relationships.

I would like to ask my readers to reflect on their relationships with their close relatives, especially brothers and sisters. Of the millions of people just in this country the closest to us are the members of our own family. The Fourth Commandment extends not just to our parents, but also to our relatives. It is a beautiful thing to see brothers and sisters who truly love one another, who are concerned about the welfare of one another, who enjoy one another's company. On the other hand, how tragic it is when brothers and sisters hate each other, will not speak to each other and perhaps even try to harm each other. Any hospital chaplain can recount sad tales of how estranged brothers and sisters try to make up while one of them is on his or her death bed—sometimes when they have not spoken to each other for twenty or thirty years. Scripture says, "Behold, how good and pleasant it is when brothers dwell in unity!" (Ps 133:1).

By the Fourth Commandment we are commanded to love our brothers and sisters, to behave well towards them, to put up with their faults (they must also learn to put up with our faults!) and to help them when we can. Older brothers and sisters should look after the younger ones. Those individuals who are born into a large family are the beneficiaries of a special blessing from God.

Relatives too are closer to us than other people, and are therefore deserving of more attention. We should at least show our affection for them and try to help them in any way we can when they are in need. "Help" in this case does not always mean money; very often it can mean a kind word, or a visit to them when they are sick, or even a card at Christmas or on the occasion of a birthday.

In the last essay we made a few observations about authority. Every one on earth is subject to some authority. Those who are legitimately in authority hold that authority not in their own name but in the name of God. We would do well to recall Jesus' words to Pontius Pilate, the Roman Governor who condemned him to death: "You would have no power over me whatever unless it were given to you from above" (Jn 19:11).

By the Fourth Commandment, therefore, we are directed to be obedient to all lawful authority. That is a very broad statement which requires many qualifications and which is very difficult to apply in many concrete situations. One clear case is the relation between teachers and students. Parents are the primary teachers of their children and have the primary responsibility for their upbringing. But in our society parents are not capable of properly educating their children, so they send them to school. In sending their children to a school the parents are sharing their authority over their children with the teachers and school authorities. In virtue of the Fourth Commandment, therefore, students have the obligation to respect and obey their teachers in those areas that pertain to the teacher's competence. Of course, we are assuming here that the teachers remain within the limits of their competence and do not violate the rights either of the parents or the students.

Another important area of human relations covered by the Fourth Commandment is the matter of respect for old people. The aged have a special dignity. In the course of their lives they have gathered great experience; many have worked very hard, have risked their lives for their country, have sacrificed for their children. It is absolutely shocking the way many old people are treated in the United States. Many live in terror—terror of being mugged or killed by teenage thugs. In New York City there are reports in the news often about violence inflicted on old people—usually by the young. One sociologist said recently that America is the first society in the history of the world in which the elderly live in fear of the young.

We should all reflect on both our attitude toward the elderly and our treatment of them. We read in the Bible (Lev 19:32): "Stand up in the presence of the aged, and show respect for the old."

24

"HE WHO SPARES THE ROD
HATES HIS SON"

In the context of the Fourth Commandment it is well to consider the obligation of parents. There is no doubt that love is the fundamental obligation of parents toward their children. All other duties are rooted in that love.

As a result of their love for each other, in the normal course of events husband and wife bring forth children and so become father and mother. Children are a gift from God—a personal gift that must be cared for in many different ways. First of all, parents must provide for the material and social needs of their children. They must feed and clothe them, look after their health, guide them into suitable work and help them plan for their future. Children must gradually be taught to be self-reliant and to provide for themselves, since parents will not always be there to care for them. When children are physically or mentally handicapped a family can be forced into severe financial difficulties. In such cases the state should assist the parents, but the ultimate responsibility for the children remains in the hands of the parents.

Parents also have a very serious obligation to look after the spiritual instruction and training of their children. As Catholic parents they should have their children baptized as soon as possible, send them to Catholic schools if that is feasible and provide for their religious instruction. But good instruction by itself is not sufficient.

Parents must also set a good example for their children, by leading virtuous Catholic lives.

In our society, Catholic family living can be very difficult and even confusing at times, since the Church in our day is plagued with internal dissent—especially with regard to obedience to our Holy Father and the bishops and with regard to the method and content of religious instruction both in the Catholic schools and in the various C.C.D. programs. The Catholic Church is going through a period of turmoil and this is being reflected in Catholic families.

A case in point is attendance at Mass on Sundays and holy days of obligation such as the Ascension or Immaculate Conception. Parents certainly have the right to require that their children who still live under their roof attend Mass on Sunday. I know, of course, that this matter is the source of many bitter disputes in some families, especially with teenage children. It can happen that the faith of a teenage son or daughter has been either destroyed or seriously weakened by various influences of our secularistic society, so much so that he or she absolutely refuses to go to church on Sunday. A prudent father or mother may decide, for the sake of harmony in the family, to tolerate this infidelity rather than force the issue to the extent that the son or daughter is driven from the home. This is a painful and delicate problem; if the parents tolerate such a situation they should do all they can to protect the faith of the younger children who could be scandalized.

Good example and instruction are commendable, but they are, by themselves alone, not sufficient for the Christian education of children. There must also be correction, admonition and, at times, punishment of children. This is so because we are not all disposed to do the right thing at all times. There is such a thing as sin and rebellion against what is good and holy. Man's inclination to evil is a constant theme of Holy Scripture and is also part of the dogmatic teaching of the Church. Human nature is essentially good, but as a result of the fall of Adam we have a tendency toward evil and are subject to temptation. Thus, St. Paul himself said that he did not do the good he wanted to do and what he did not want to do—that is what he did. Accordingly, the loving parent will correct his erring children. However, admonition and punishment should always be just, should proceed from love and should not be carried out in a fit of anger. In this regard we read the wise words in Proverbs (13:24): "He who spares the rod hates his son, but he who loves him is diligent to discipline him."

St. Paul writes in Ephesians (6:4): "Fathers, do not provoke your children to anger, but bring them up in the discipline and instruction of the Lord." That one sentence summarizes the main points of the present essay. In another letter Paul tells parents not to nag their children. Thus, there is a difference between a just correction that proceeds from love and a neurotic "nagging" that manifests character deficiencies in the parent. By the Fourth Commandment, then, parents are directed to love and care for their children to the best of their ability and according to the measure of divine grace given to them.

25

CAESAR AND GOD

The Fourth Commandment does more than just regulate relations between children and parents. Since it is the one commandment that is directly concerned with the role of authority in the human community, the relations between the individual and the state are also commonly treated in moral theology under the heading of the Fourth Commandment.

It is firmly established in Catholic philosophy and theology that the state or political community is a natural entity, that is, it flows from the requirements of human nature and therefore is willed by God. Another way of saying the same thing is to assert that the natural law requires the existence of the state. The state has as its object the promotion of the common good of all its citizens or subjects. In order to achieve its end the state must be able to command certain acts or to forbid them. In order to command or forbid, the state must be endowed with authority. Since God wills the existence of the state and since the state cannot function without some authority, it follows that the authority of the state comes from God. Thus, in reply to Pontius Pilate's question, "Do you not know that I have power to release you, and power to crucify you?" Jesus replied, "You would have no power over me unless it had been given you from above" (Jn 19:10–11). Jesus thereby indicates the divine source of authority, even as that authority exists in a pagan state such as the Roman Empire of the time.

On another occasion, when Jesus was asked about paying taxes, he said: "Render to Caesar the things that are Caesar's, and to God the things that are God's" (Lk 20:25). St. Paul told the Romans that they were conscience bound to obey the secular authorities in the passage that begins with the words: "Let every person be subject to the governing authorities. For there is no authority except from God, and those that exist have been instituted by God" (Rom 13:1–7).

I would like to point out here that authority is moral power over the will of another—a power that can direct another either to do something or to refrain from something. Since it is a "moral" power, it is or can be binding in conscience. Since authority comes from God there is something sacred about it and so it should be treated with respect both by those who exercise it and those who are subject to it.

If we apply the above to the state we can draw a number of immediate and practical conclusions. Thus, state officials are obliged to use their authority for the common good and to promote justice in all of their activities. This means that they must provide for the general welfare, avert harm as much as possible, avoid favoritism and refrain from taking bribes. Elected officials such as congressmen must participate in the deliberations of the government and they must vote against evil legislation. In our day this becomes very urgent, since Catholic legislators are duty bound to oppose such things as abortion, experimentation on live fetuses and euthanasia.

The Fourth Commandment requires that citizens love

their country, be sincerely interested in its welfare and respect and obey its lawful authority. A person who plots against his own country or rebels against its legitimate government can be guilty of a grave sin against God and neighbor. Of course, citizens have a right to defend themselves against tyranny when there is no other way to secure the exercise of their fundamental human rights.

Citizens should exercise their right to vote. Voting could be a matter of serious obligation if the common good of the state or of religion or of the innocent lives of others were involved. Citizens of a country as well as aliens should obey the law of paying just taxes in order to contribute their fair share to the lawful expenses of good government and public security. On the other hand, state officials have an obligation not to waste taxpayers' money on useless, dishonest or extravagant programs.

Citizens are also obliged to help their country wage a just war of defense. They must serve in the armed forces if the government commands them to do so, unless they are convinced from adequate and unquestionable evidence that the war is unjust.

Finally, we must respect and obey the lawful authority of our country because it comes from God who is the source of all authority. But we must remember that the state exists for the good of men, and not men for the state. A state may not infringe on the natural human rights of individuals or families. And if a government commands citizens to violate the law of God they must refuse to obey, heeding the words of St. Peter and the Apostles, "We must obey God rather than men" (Acts 5:29).

26

MAN'S UNALIENABLE RIGHT TO LIFE

The Fifth Commandment is, "You shall not kill" (Ex 20:13). There are very many ramifications of God's commandment to respect life, especially today in our society when there are so many threats against human life on all sides: biological, sociological, political, environmental, economical and medical.

The Catholic Christian accepts as a datum of faith that a personal God exists and that that God created, by a free act of his will, the world and everything that is in the entire universe. God's creation is good, desirable and to be respected: "God saw all he had made, and indeed it was very good" (Gen 1:31).

The pinnacle of God's material creation is man who in some way actually mirrors the Lord God himself, for "God created man in the image of himself, in the image of God he created him, male and female he created them" (Gen 1:27).

Without going into the whole of Bible history, suffice it to say that man is much more than a material, biological being who lives out his "three score and ten" years on this earth and then returns, like the beasts of the forest, to the dust and slime from which he was taken. No. Man has an eternal destiny. He has an immortal soul that is destined for eternal happiness in a most personal, intimate union of knowledge and love with God forever.

Since man was created in the image and likeness of God and since he has an eternal destiny, he has an importance that goes far beyond his usefulness and functions in this life. Because of man's special relationship with God, he is endowed by God with certain "unalienable rights", that is, God-given rights that antedate the state and are not derived from the state. Thus, it is obvious even from the study of history and cultural anthropology that the family and the tribe or clan were in existence for thousands of years before the advent of the historical states and empires. Man was in possession of rights therefore before the arrival of the state with its courts and police force which have been erected to protect those rights.

The first and most important of all man's natural rights is his right to life, for if his life is taken away then all other rights become meaningless. All other rights of man are based on his unalienable right to life. The Lord gives and the Lord takes away. In the Christian view of the world God is the source of all life; he is also the Master of life. He gives it and only he can justly and legitimately take it away. This means then that, according to the Christian worldview, no human person, no organization and no state agency has the right to dispose arbitrarily of human life. Often we use the word "sacred" to characterize God and those things closely associated with him. Because of man's close association with God perhaps it is best to describe his life as "sacred". When so designated it means that man is to keep his hands off human life—at least in the sense of trying to dispose of it for his own selfish purposes.

Accordingly, God forbids one man to kill another, as happened in the case of the first recorded murder when Cain slew his brother Abel (Gen 4:8). In the tradition of the Church and in the explanations of the theologians, this Commandment has always been understood in the sense of "You shall not commit murder," murder being here understood in the sense of the *unjust* killing of another. Certainly the Commandment does not apply to the killing of animals as a source of food supply. It directly concerns the killing of other human beings. However, both the Bible and the tradition of the Church affirm the liceity and morality of killing another human being in certain, well-defined circumstances, such as killing an unjust aggressor against oneself or against a third party who is innocent, or the killing that is involved in a just, defensive war.

Sometimes complete pacifists appeal to this Commandment as a total prohibition against all killing, even of the unjust aggressor. There is no justification for such an argument either in the tradition of the Church or in the doctrine of the great Fathers and theologians of the Church. It is certainly not Catholic teaching that a heavily armed, murderous psychopath, who is shooting down innocent people, may not be stopped even if it is necessary to kill him in order to stop him.

27

STEWARDS OF LIFE

It is clear from the first chapters of the Book of Genesis that God is the author of human life: he created Adam and his wife Eve and commanded them to increase and multiply. "The Lord God formed man of dust from the ground, and breathed into his nostrils the breath of life; and man became a living being" (Gen 2:7). God not only gives life; he also protects it through his Commandment: "You shall not kill." There are many aspects to this Commandment. One of them is man's positive duty to preserve his life to the best of his ability and according to the dictates of reason.

The profound difference in outlook between Catholics and all types of atheists and materialists stands out sharply in the matter of respect for human life. For the pragmatic atheist/materialist human life is basically a natural resource like fresh water or crude oil; it is to be used for the betterment of the state or human society. For them, when human life becomes "useless", in the sense that it does not contribute to the G.N.P. in some way, it is to be eliminated the same way one disposes of garbage. This mentality explains the attitude of atheistic materialists in questions of abortion, infanticide and mercy killing. Since for them man is the only absolute, it is up to man alone to decide who shall live and who shall die.

The Catholic view of human life is worlds apart from that of the atheistic secular humanists. For the Catholic, human life is sacred, it is inviolable, because it was given by God almighty. And not only did God bestow on us human life, but he also, by an absolutely free act of love, raised man to the supernatural level and so destined him for eternal life in the beatific, face-to-face vision of God. Because men have a supernatural destiny as the adopted children of God and heirs of heaven, they have a dignity that is innate and that surpasses any honor that can be conferred by this world. In the concrete, this means that no one may "use" human life for his own selfish purposes, whether it be for the good of the state or for the progress of science.

Since life is a gift from God, we are not absolute masters of our own lives. It is more accurate to say that we are "stewards" or "caretakers" of our lives and that God will demand from us an accounting of our stewardship. We did not cause ourselves or bring ourselves into existence.

Why did God give life to man? He gave man life so that he might grow in the knowledge and love of God, practice virtue and merit eternal life with the help of God's grace. God in his providence allots a certain amount of time to each one of us in order to accomplish the purpose for which he created us. In order to "work out our salvation in fear and trembling" we need first of all to live so that we can respond to God's loving Word. This being the case, as a good steward man must take care of his life, using all of the ordinary means put at his disposal by God. It is contrary to the will of God, and therefore sinful, unreasonably to injure one's body or to shorten one's life.

For centuries Catholic moral theologians have stressed the fact that man is morally obliged to use the ordinary means to preserve his life, but that he is not obliged to use extraordinary means. The principle is clear, but it is not always easy to discern what is an "ordinary" means and what is an "extraordinary" means. In general, all measures which will impose no more than a reasonable hardship on us are considered *ordinary* and therefore obligatory.

> Included in this category would be not only normal food, drink and rest, but also all medicines, treatments and operations

which offer a reasonable hope of benefit for the patient and which can be used without excessive expense, pain, or other grave hardship (C. J. McFadden, *The Dignity of Life*, O.S.V., 1976, 149).

It is worth repeating that it is morally binding on all men to use the ordinary means of preserving life. However, the natural moral law does not require a person to use means which would involve a grave hardship. These are called "extraordinary means" and are therefore not compulsory or morally binding.

In this category would be all medicines, treatments and operations which cannot be obtained or used without excessive expense, pain, or other grave hardship for the patient or for others, or which, if used, would not offer a reasonable hope of benefit to the patient (McFadden, 150).

Until very recently it was not particularly difficult for moralists to say which means were ordinary and which were extraordinary. But with the rapid development of medical science in the past forty years, this matter has become increasingly complex and difficult. The principle is clear but the application is often obscure in particular cases. The Karen Quinlan case is a good example of what I mean. Moralists were divided in their opinion on whether or not the use of a respirator for her was an ordinary means of treatment or an extraordinary means.

28

THE CATHOLIC CHURCH
AND EUTHANASIA

By his Fifth Commandment, "You shall not kill," God forbids the destruction of all innocent human life. Since the prohibition is absolute, it means that all murder, abortion, euthanasia or "mercy killing" and suicide are forbidden by God and are therefore immoral and sinful. In this essay I want to say a few things about euthanasia.

Most Catholics and practicing Christians were shocked at the rapidity with which permissive abortion swept our country and finally became the law of the land in January 1973. With that victory under their belts, the pro-abortion forces moved quickly to concentrate their efforts on the promotion of euthanasia, which is also called "mercy killing" or the direct, painless killing of the defective, the insane, the aged and the incurably ill. Thus the campaign for "death with dignity" is now in full swing. Unless all Christians and God-fearing people resist the movement, I fully expect to see permissive euthanasia laws enacted in this country within the next five years.

Reports from various parts of America indicate that a limited type of euthanasia is already being practiced. An organization located in Fort Lauderdale, called "American Euthanasia Foundation, Inc.", already has plans for a "Mercy Hospice" to be located somewhere in the Western Hemisphere. The facility will be called "The Heavenly Rest" and will euthanatize anyone who can pay for the entire package. The planned "low cost" service will include special (one way) air travel, pleasant accomodations, three days of spiritual counseling, application of the painless, fast-acting and killing pill called "Evipan", plus cremation for those who so desire.

Since euthanasia is the unjust killing of an innocent person, it is murder and so is strictly forbidden by the Fifth Commandment. Although I have not yet heard the argument, I have no doubt that we will soon be told, as we are now constantly lectured by the anti-life crowd, that Catholics and Christians have no right to "impose their own morality" on the rest of the nation by supporting and enforcing laws that forbid euthanasia. Of course, it should be noted, the very same people have no qualms of conscience about imposing *their* morality (?) on us.

When we talk about euthanasia and "death with dignity" we must be careful to know precisely what is at issue. What the law of God forbids is the *direct* killing of an innocent human being, whether healthy or unhealthy. In the matter of euthanasia this means that no positive or active steps may be taken to terminate the life of another; thus, no shooting, no lethal injections or pills, no air injected into the arteries, and so forth. It also requires that all of the *ordinary* means of sustaining life must be used until a sick person dies of natural causes; this includes normal food, drink, rest, medicines and treatments that do not involve a grave hardship.

However, there is no moral obligation to employ *extraordinary* means to preserve life; this is so when a patient is aged, comotose and terminally ill. Sometimes such a situation is called "passive euthanasia". This means simply that nature is allowed to take its course, without the application of some of the modern marvels of medical science. Passive euthanasia in this sense is not against the Fifth Commandment and, in fact, has been allowed in Catholic hospitals for decades. But *active* or *direct* euthanasia is murder.

As in the matter of abortion, in the question of the moral permissibility of active euthanasia one's position is ultimately determined by his or her view of man and God. The secular humanist who denies God and places man at the pinnacle of the universe looks upon active euthanasia as a social good, since, in his view, the defective, aged and incurably ill cannot make positive contributions to human society and cannot enhance the G.N.P. He sees no purpose whatsoever in suffering; for him, to kill the suffering, terminally ill cancer patient is an act of human compassion and kindness.

The Catholic Church recognizes God as the Creator and master of human life—man is merely a custodian of that life. Since man is created in the image and likeness of God his life is sacred. The Lord gives and the Lord takes away; blessed be the name of the Lord. In God's plan human life extends beyond death into eternity. Though we do not fully understand suffering and death, as Christians we follow Christ and try to imitate him as best we can. The main thing is to find and to obey God's will, just as Jesus did. Euthanasia, whether as suicide or murder, is a flagrant act of disobedience against God's most holy will.

29

INNOCENT HUMAN LIFE

The Fifth Commandment of God enjoins respect for human life at all stages of its existence, from conception to death. Most God-fearing Americans were shocked at the rapidity with which permissive abortion swept the country in the late 1960s and early 1970s, only to become the law of the land through the infamous Supreme Court decision of January 22, 1973. It should be clear by now to all but the most obtuse that the Catholic Church utterly condemns direct abortion, no matter what motive, good or bad, may be adduced for it. For, direct abortion is the deliberate taking of innocent human life and that is murder no matter how you slice it.

The matter has been exhaustively treated in the Catholic press, so I do not intend here to belabor the obvious. But since abortion is forbidden by the Fifth Commandment, it will not be out of place to make a few observations about it.

Condemnation of abortion as murder has been the constant teaching of the Roman Catholic Church since the first century. For example, the *Didache*, which was composed before 80 A.D. and enjoyed great authority in the early Church, states: "You shall not procure abortion. You shall not destroy a newborn child." The same teaching can be found in the writings of the Fathers —Clement of Alexandria, Origen, Jerome, Chrysostom, Augustine, and the most recent popes from Pius XI to John Paul II. The basic reason why Catholics obey this teaching is the authority conferred on her in Peter and the Apostles by Jesus Christ himself to teach in his name.

When speaking about abortion we should be careful to be precise in the use of language. "Abortion" as understood in Catholic morality means expelling an immature fetus from the mother's womb. If abortion happens spontaneously or if the fetus dies in the womb, then there is no question of a moral fault. The sin of abortion is involved in expelling a live fetus that is immature or nonviable.

With the legislation of abortion the term is also used to describe what is strictly speaking a form of "feticide", that is, killing the fetus in the womb by physical or chemical means, such as the use of a suction pump or a saline injection or curettage. All such procedures result in the death of an innocent human being and are strictly forbidden by the Church. In fact, the Church is so concerned about the evil of direct abortion that she has attached a penalty of excommunication on anyone who performs an abortion, undergoes an abortion or even counsels another person to have an abortion. However, the sin of abortion is not involved in certain types of surgical procedures, directly undertaken to save the life of a woman who happens to be pregnant, one of whose results is the death of a fetus. Examples of this are the removal of an ectopic pregnancy (i.e., tubal pregnancy) and the removal of a diseased uterus after the beginning of a pregnancy. In such cases the death of the fetus is not directly willed, but is permitted. What is directly willed is the health of the woman.

The essential evil and sinfulness of direct abortion consists in the homicidal intent to kill innocent human life. Precisely when the soul is infused, whether at conception (which is most likely) or some time later, is irrelevant. For, whoever is guilty of a direct abortion is willing to kill what is or may be a human person. Biologically there is no doubt that the blastocyst/embryo/fetus is alive from conception; it is most probable that the human soul is created by God and infused into the matter at the moment of conception. The fetus is either human or it is not and it is impossible to prove that it becomes "human" at some point in the process of gestation. Since the end product of the whole process is a new human being, the principle of finality would seem to require that it is human from the first moment of its existence. For there is no such thing as being more human or less human. So anyone who destroys the fruit of the womb at any stage of its development is guilty of murder by intent.

The Second Vatican Council reiterated the constant tradition of the Church when it declared in the Constitution on the Church in the Modern World: "Life must be protected with the utmost care from the moment of conception: abortion and infanticide are abominable crimes" (51). Pope Paul VI said in 1974 in his Declaration on Abortion: "Respect for human life is called for from the time that the ovum is fertilized, a life is begun which is neither that of the father nor of the mother. . . . Divine law and natural reason exclude all right to the direct killing of an innocent human being."

30

MUTILATION AND STERILIZATION

By the Fifth Commandment we are commanded to take proper care of our own bodily well-being and that of our neighbor. In the normal course of life we obey this commandment by taking reasonable care of our health and by respecting the life and good health of others. In addition to forbidding murder, suicide, euthanasia, and so forth, this commandment also forbids all unnecessary and unnatural mutilation of the body.

In view of recent papal teaching and in the light of the advances of modern medicine, we may define *mutilation* as any procedure that either temporarily or permanently impairs the natural and complete integrity of the body or its functions. Basic to any question of mutilation is the theological fact that our right of dominion over our lives and bodies is only a limited right. As a creature of God, man is custodian, not proprietor of his body, and consequently he may dispose of his life and bodily members only within the limited scope of their natural finality as established by God.

However, since the parts of the body are at the service of the whole, one may sacrifice a diseased member of the body in order to preserve the life and health of the whole. Thus, one is morally justified in amputating a diseased arm or leg, in removing a cancerous lung or uterus, and so forth. In this regard Pope Pius XII made use of what he called "the principle of totality" in order to justify the moral licitness of amputations and other mutilations.

In our day the matter of the morality of mutilation has become quite acute in the area of sterilization—here understood not in the general sense of freeing some object from germ life, but in the more restricted sense of impeding or removing the germ cell potential of the reproductive system in either a man or a woman. Since sterilization is a form of mutilation it must be judged according to the moral norms that govern the latter.

As a surgical or chemical or irradiation procedure, sterilization in itself can be either good or evil depending on the circumstances and the intention behind the act. As a general principle we can say that *direct sterilization* that is undertaken for contraceptive or eugenic reasons is intrinsically evil and so forbidden by the law of God. By "direct sterilization" is meant any procedure whose purpose is to render a man or woman incapable of generating offspring. Direct sterilization of this kind has been practiced extensively in India and was legally imposed on the people in certain parts of the country. Forced sterilization was so unpopular that it contributed to the defeat and downfall of Indira Ghandi's government. The new Indian government promised to do away with forced sterilization and return to a more lenient policy of voluntary sterilization. But from the point of view of Christian morality, direct sterilization is sinful whether it is forced or voluntary, since man is not the absolute master of his reproductive faculty.

According to the principle of totality, however, it is morally allowable, and sometimes required, to undergo a medical treatment that will result in sterility. Such a situation occurs when the generative faculties are diseased and will become a threat to the health of the whole organism if all or part of them is not removed or treated either chemically or by irradiation with x-rays. A few examples would be the removal of the womb (hysterectomy) or testicles (orchiectomy) when these organs are the site of malignant tumors, or the suppression of ovarian function by x-ray irradiation, or the ligation of the ducts through which the male sperm cells enter the ejaculate (vasectomy) when these ducts are the site of some serious retrograde infection. However, none of these procedures may be undertaken with contraceptive or eugenic intent. To be morally licit, the direct intent of these and similar procedures must be the well-being of the whole body; when sterility results from such procedures, from a moral point of view, it is *indirect sterilization*.

In addition to the above-described and morally licit therapeutic sterilization, today many reasons are advanced in support of widespread, direct sterilization. The most common reasons advanced are overpopulation, protection of the environment, improving the standard of living and the quality of the human race. No matter how legitimate these goals may be in certain circumstances, a good end never justifies the use of evil means to attain it. And direct, contraceptive sterilization is an evil means that can never be morally justified.

31

MORALITY OF A JUST WAR

In the last few chapters we have discussed some of the implications and requirements of the Fifth Commandment, "You shall not kill." Now I would like to touch briefly on the morality of war. War has been very much a gruesome companion to that segment of mankind that has lived and is now living in the twentieth century. Many of us carry vivid memories of the Vietnam war. Currently there is some fighting in Southern Africa, with a threat of a wider conflict there in the very near future. However, overshadowing all such minor struggles is the ever-present danger of a major nuclear exchange between Russia and the United States—a war, probably lasting only a few hours or days, that could destroy Western civilization and make the world a vast graveyard.

It is not pleasant to talk about the possibility of nuclear war, but since it is a definite possibility we must face up to it. So we must ask the hard question: Is it morally permissible for the Catholic Christian to engage in nuclear war? The complete pacifist will reply: No, war under any and all circumstances is immoral, since it is absolutely forbidden to kill another. If he is correct then the whole defense system of the United States is contrary to the will of God and therefore immoral. Logically, he must say that we should destroy all our weapons and throw ourselves at the mercy of the Russians and the Chinese. Although there are some few Catholics who hold this position following in the footsteps of Tertullian and Origen, the Catholic Church has never taught or embraced complete pacifism. Even though the Second Vatican Council denounced "total war", it recognized the right of sovereign states to arm themselves for defense: "As long as the danger of war remains and there is no competent and sufficiently powerful authority at the international level, governments cannot be denied the right to legitimate defense once every means of peaceful settlement has been exhausted" (*The Church Today*, 79).

Since the time of St. Augustine in the fifth century Catholic moralists have defended the "just war theory". The requirements for a just war, as laid down by St. Thomas Aquinas, are three: 1) it must be waged by public authority (not by private groups); 2) the cause must be just; 3) there must be a right intention, for example, to secure justice and peace for the populace. Later theologians added two more conditions: 4) it must be fought as a last resort after all other means of resolving the conflict have been exhausted, and 5) in the proper manner, i.e., without destruction of the innocent.

The above analysis of a just war was very common among Catholic moralists up until World War II and the advent of obliteration bombing and the atomic bomb. Formerly, it was held that, if the above conditions were fulfilled, it was morally permissible not only to defend oneself from an unjust aggressor, but also to initiate a war against another state in order to reclaim some lost right, such as territory, oil wells, etc. However, since modern technology has so dramatically increased the destructiveness of war, few if any theologians would today try to defend the moral liceity of an offensive war in order to secure some "right". The reason is that the destruction and loss of life would be all out of proportion to the good to be obtained by such a course of action.

But many Catholic moralists defend the moral liceity of waging a defensive war against an unjust aggressor, especially if that aggressor intends to destroy the freedom and whole way of life of the state attacked. Such a situation could arise between the United States and Russia. Experts report alarming increases in the Russian production of the most sophisticated and advanced weapons in recent years. If Russia suddenly moves to take West Berlin or Western Europe—and there is little doubt that they have the capacity to do it—what will the United States do? An attack against them is an attack against us. If all efforts at averting war have been exhausted, Pope Pius XII said in 1957 "a war of efficacious self-defense against unjust attacks, which is undertaken with hope of success, cannot be considered illicit."

The moral problem in evaluating the liceity of modern nuclear warfare is whether or not it can be *limited*, since total war of one people against another is morally indefensible. For, in total war there are no non-combatants, that is, every man, woman and child in the hostile country is considered a legitimate target for destruction. Such a view has always been rejected by the Church, since the Fifth Commandment forbids the killing of the innocent. On this point Vatican II said: "Any act of war aimed indiscriminately at the destruction of entire cities or of extensive areas along with their population is a crime against God and man himself. It merits unequivocal and unhesitating condemnation" (*The Church Today*, 80). So even a just defensive war must be limited to attacking only the military forces of the enemy. If innocent people are killed in the defense then it must be only indirectly and not as the result of a direct attack against them. The moral justification of engaging in modern warfare requires that there be some hope of success and that there be a proportionate reason for doing so, i.e., the desired good must exceed the expected evil and destruction.

If it could be shown for certain that limited nuclear war is impossible, that is, that any use of nuclear weapons *necessarily* leads to total war, then the Catholic would have to hold that nuclear war is essentially evil and therefore always and in all circumstances forbidden. Up till now that position has not been conclusively demonstrated.

32

ADEQUATE CARE OF ONE'S HEALTH

It is more or less obvious to most Catholics that the Fifth Commandment covers such things as murder, mutilation, abortion, sterilization, suicide and war. It may not be so obvious to many that the Fifth Commandment also extends to the preservation of life and health. The reason is that death can result from the neglect of adequate care of one's health. With this essay then I would like to conclude our consideration of the Fifth Commandment by making a few observations on eating, drinking, smoking and taking drugs.

In a previous essay I pointed out that man does not have absolute dominion over his life, since it comes from God and is to be used according to God's law. Man is the steward of his life. He is to care for his body so that he can live a fully human life worthy of a child of God. St. Ignatius Loyola over four hundred years ago stressed that man was created to praise, reverence and serve God and in this way to save his soul.

As we have seen, we are morally bound to use the *ordinary* means of preserving our life. Such means include proper food, clothing, housing, common remedies, and so forth. We are not bound to use *extraordinary* means which impose a severe burden and tend to be unusual.

Adequate care of one's health is directly related to moderation in all things. Moderation is a requirement of the cardinal virtue of temperance. Of course, it applies to everything a person does, but in the present context it has a special relevance to restraint in eating and drinking.

The general principle here is simple, though it is not always simple to apply it to concrete cases. The principle is that one should not deliberately do anything that would injure his health or shorten his life. The moral theologians say that gluttony, or overeating, is a venial sin. Rarely do we come across people who eat so much that they become sick, but there is no doubt that there is much overeating in our affluent society. High calorie intake with little physical activity results in obesity for most people. Thousands of people in the United States die each year from heart failure and many heart attacks are directly related to overweight and overeating. It is not easy to lay down a moral norm in this matter. However, one can sin by self-indulgence in the matter of food, especially if it is so excessive that it damages one's health.

Intemperance with regard to alcoholic beverages is a much more serious question. For, food and ordinary drink are necessary to sustain life, whereas alcoholic drinks are not at all necessary. Drunkenness of its very nature is a serious sin since it deprives a person of his or her rationality and debases human dignity. That is the moral dimension of drunkenness. There is also the physical side of it, since alcoholism seriously impairs health and often leads to an early death. Alcohol is especially dangerous for the pregnant woman, since the ingestion of three to five ounces of liquor, according to a study conducted at the University of Washington, can cause permanent brain damage in the child she is carrying. That being the case, it would seem to me that a pregnant woman should avoid all alcohol.

There is a great deal of dispute and doubt about the moral liceity of smoking. There is no doubt now that excessive smoking can be, and often is, injurious to health. However, it is not easy to say precisely what "excessive" smoking means in every case. What is excessive for one (a child or teenager) may not be excessive for a healthy adult. Some smokers live to a ripe old age. Of course, there are different types of smoking, such as cigarettes, cigars, pipe, each with a different effect on the system. The amount of smoke inhaled is also a factor. But it seems to me clear that heavy smoking that is injurious to one's health is forbidden by the Fifth Commandment.

Narcotics such as opium, morphine, heroine, etc. are much more dangerous than tobacco. They produce radical changes in the body and, for the addict, often lead to an early death. Moderate usage under the direction of a physician for physical or psychological reasons is morally allowed, but addiction for the sake of pleasure or "release" is strictly forbidden. Those who are addicted to drugs and alcohol are morally obliged to abstain from the use altogether. With the exception of certain types of addicts, total abstention from alcohol and tobacco cannot be imposed as binding in conscience.

33

SEX IS SACRED

There is perhaps no area of modern life, especially in the post-Christian West, where the opposition between Catholic faith and practice on the one hand, and contemporary values and mores on the other, is more evident than it is in the whole area of sex. To put the matter very simply, for the loyal Catholic sex is sacred because it was created by God for the purpose of transmitting human life; for American pagans and secularized Christians, sex is for fun—it is a source of play and self-gratification for the autonomous person who uses it where, when and how he or she wishes with no reference whatsoever to a God-Creator.

For the most part, although not always, the basic position one takes on sex will be an indication of one's values and practice in such matters as adultery, fornication, masturbation, homosexuality, pornography, artificial contraception, and so forth. The believer will regulate his thinking and life in accordance with the laws of God and the teaching of the Church; the American pagan will think and live on the basis of "personal conscience" and popular cultural standards as set by the media and the peer group.

God said to the Israelites of old, "You shall not commit adultery" (Ex 20:14; Dt 5:18). As it was understood in the Old Testament, adultery was primarily a violation of justice, since by adultery the rights of a third party are usurped. Jesus elevated the relationship between a man and his wife to a higher level than it had been under the old law. He also made it very clear that adultery, and even adulterous thoughts are contrary to the virtue of chastity. For, we read in St. Matthew (5:27–28): "You have heard it was said to the ancients, 'You shall not commit adultery.' But I say to you that anyone who so much as looks with lust at a woman has already committed adultery with her in his heart."

It is clear that the Sixth Commandment explicitly forbids adultery, which is an act of sexual intercourse between a married man and a woman not his wife, or between a married woman and a man not her husband. The specific characteristic of the sin of adultery is that at least one of the parties is married; if neither party engaging in sexual intercourse is married the sin is called "fornication". Adultery adds a sin against justice to the intrinsically grave malice of fornication, which in itself is a misuse of the sexual faculties. It should be obvious that

216

the victim of the injustice is the innocent spouse whose marital rights are violated by the sinning parties.

Implicitly the Sixth Commandment also forbids all impurity and immodesty in words, looks and actions, whether alone or with others. What do we mean by impurity or unchastity? Impurity is any deliberate thought, word, look or deed with oneself or another by which the sexual appetite is aroused outside of marriage, and even in marriage when contrary to the purpose for which God instituted the married state. Some of the chief sins against purity are adultery, fornication, deliberate actions with oneself or others performed to arouse the sexual appetite, such as masturbation or homosexuality. Deliberately indulging in pornography of any kind should also be added here.

Modesty is a virtue which is very closely related to purity or chastity—its purpose is to protect chastity, as it were to build up defenses around it. Modesty is the moral virtue that moderates and controls the impulse for sexual display in men and women. Thus, looked at from the negative point of view, immodesty is any deliberate thought, word or action that tends toward impurity. Sins against modesty include such things as looks, touches, conversation, songs, reading, suggestive clothing, and so forth.

From the positive side, by the Sixth Commandment we are commanded to be pure and modest in our behavior. Purity (or chastity) is a moral virtue which rightly regulates all voluntary expression of sexual pleasure in marriage and excludes it altogether outside the married state. Purity also contributes very much to the preservation and strengthening of the other virtues.

Until very recently all Catholic moral theologians

taught that a fully deliberate sin of impurity is a mortal sin. In recent years some Catholic moralists seem to have retreated from this position, or else they have held that what was formerly thought to be sinful (for example, premarital sex or fornication) in all cases is now considered not sinful in some restricted cases. But what some theologians teach is not necessarily what the Catholic Church teaches. For, the Declaration from Rome, issued in December 1975, makes it very clear that fornication, masturbation and homosexuality, knowingly and willingly indulged in, are mortal sins.

34

SEX AND HUMAN LIFE

When I was studying moral theology in the seminary a number of years ago, a shrewd old professor who had himself published many books on various theological topics used to tell us over and over again: "Don't worry about theft; study and master the Sixth Commandment. That's where you will encounter most of your difficulties in the confessional." That advice was the fruit of much experience and it contained a great deal of truth.

The sexual instinct in man and woman is very strong indeed. If it were not, very few men and women, it seems to me, would voluntarily assume the rights and obligations of the married state, thereby committing themselves to each other for life and committing themselves to raising the children that God might send them. Human beings are also very weak. Their weakness is especially evident in violations of the Sixth Commandment—as our old professor intimated. In fact, sexual sins are so common that the word "immorality", which can rightly be applied to violations against all the commandments, now most commonly refers to sins against the Sixth Commandment.

Man's weakness in the face of his powerful sexual instinct has led some moral philosophers, and even some Christians, to look upon sex and sexual intercourse as something evil. Such an attitude is contrary to the teaching of the Bible and the constant tradition of the Church. At the very beginning of the Bible we read: "God created man in the image of himself, in the image of God he created him, male and female he created them. God blessed them, saying to them, 'Be fruitful, multiply, fill the earth and conquer it' " (Gen 1:27–28). Thus the sexual organs are good and the sexual act in marriage is also good, because of its two-fold God-given purpose: the generation of children and as an expression of committed love between husband and wife.

There is no escaping the fact that sex is essentially related to the transmission of human life. Since human life comes from God in a special way, it enjoys a certain inviolability—it is sacred. In the generation of children, man and wife are cooperating with the creative power of God in a very special way. Most Catholic theologians have held that each human soul is immediately created by God at the moment of conception. Pope Pius XII, in his encyclical *Humani Generis*, taught: "The Catholic faith obliges us to hold firmly that souls are immediately created by God" (*D* 3027).

Because of its relationship to human life, the Church has always considered sex important. In accordance with Scripture, she has always insisted that the love and service of God cannot be reconciled with adultery, fornication, promiscuity, lustful desires (cf. Mt 5:28), self-abuse, homosexual acts and other sexual perversions. Such acts violate the basic human good involved in the proper use of the sex faculty and so are a misuse of God's generous gifts. In a word, they are seriously sinful because they run contrary to man's true good as revealed in the Bible and also as known through the use of human reason (cf. Rom 1).

According to the Bible and the constant teaching of the Church, sexual intercourse is a moral good only within the context of marriage. This is a hard saying and it is very difficult for many people to understand. Why, we are often asked, is pre-marital sex not morally permissible if the couple truly love each other? The Church replies by saying that sexual intercourse represents and expresses a permanent, mutual gift of self which is realized only in marriage. Here, obviously, we are touching on the *symbolic* nature of the sex act, since in human persons sex is not just a mechanical, strictly biological activity. For, sexual intercourse between a man and a woman gives exterior expression to the interior love that exists between them. If it is not an expression of love, then it is a form of violence, such as rape, or some type of prostitution.

The permanence and monogamous nature of marriage are based, in Catholic thinking, on two factors: the education of children to maturity and the growth of love and friendship between a man and his wife. It does not take very long to conceive and bear children, but it is a long process to raise them and educate them to maturity. But even after children have reached adulthood they still need and depend on their parents in many ways. Also, growth in love and mutual self-giving takes a lifetime. Accordingly, sexual activity must be confined to marriage and marriage, in Catholic teaching, is both monogamous and indissoluble. This teaching, I know, is commonly rejected today by American pagans, but that does not make it any less true.

35

TWO IN ONE FLESH

The fundamental opposition between Catholicism and contemporary paganism or materialism or secularism —or whatever you want to call it—is becoming more evident, almost with each passing day. True, there are many ecclesiastics and Catholic intellectuals who are trying hard to show that there is no basic conflict between the Catholic Church and the trends of modern society. Their best efforts, in my opinion, will come to naught. There can be no compromise for the faithful Catholic in the matter of killing the unborn, direct sterilization, the direct killing of the aged and infirm (the present goal of the euthanasia lobby).

One point of Catholic teaching that stands in open contradiction to the modern permissive mentality is that of the absolute prohibition of divorce and remarriage. It should be obvious, even to the casual observer, that there has been a significant breakdown in family life in America in the course of the past hundred years. During that time there has been a change from an almost universal social condemnation of divorce/remarriage to widespread acceptance of it. According to recent studies, four out of every ten marriages in the U.S. end up in divorce. In some parts of the country, one out of every two marriages ends up in disaster. Among teenagers the rate is even higher.

Like Christ himself, the Catholic Church is a sign of contradiction. While the law, the media, the intellectuals, and most of the churches in this country approve of divorce/remarriage, the Catholic Church says: No. A sacramental marriage between baptized Christians, validly performed and duly consummated after the reception of the Sacrament of Matrimony, is indissoluble by any authority on earth. It is certain and official Catholic teaching that such marriages image the covenant love that Jesus has for his Church—a love that is both permanent and sacrificial (see Eph 5:21–33). Just as Jesus gave himself up for his Church and loves her with an eternal love, so also is the commitment of husband to wife and wife to husband an enduring bond. And just as no one can separate Christ from his Church, so also no one can break a sacramental bond of marriage.

This is admittedly a difficult teaching, but one that the Church has always proclaimed and defended. Let us not forget that all of England was lost to Rome because the Pope refused to allow Henry VIII to divorce and re-marry. Each year in this country tens of thousands of Catholics either leave the Church or are excluded from the sacraments because they abandon their spouses, for one reason or another, and then "remarry" outside the Church. Such so-called "marriages", as any Catholic should know who is schooled in the rudiments of the faith, are not really marriages since the divorced Catholic party is not free to marry anyone else as long as he or she is held by the first valid bond of marriage.

Without doubt, there is much that the Church can do to help those whose marriages have ended in failure. In recent years diocesan marriage tribunals have been given much more authority in the handling of marriage cases where there may be some doubt about the validity of the first marriage. In 1965 there were about five hundred declarations of nullity in the whole country; in 1976 there were over fifteen thousand.

You may know someone who was married in the Church, then divorced, then allowed to marry again in the Catholic Church. Some people seem to think that the Catholic Church now practices a limited form of divorce. If they do, they are in error. Divorce was repudiated by the Council of Trent, by Pius XI, by Pius XII and by the Second Vatican Council. That is the constant teaching of the Church and cannot be changed. But declarations of nullity are another matter. Such declarations involve a pronouncement by Church authority that a particular marriage, even though perhaps performed twenty-five years ago with due solemnity and followed by numerous children and many years of living together, was not a valid marriage for one reason

223

or another. Some of the acceptable reasons are homo-sexuality, fear, ignorance of the nature of marriage and so forth.

But the fact that diocesan marriage tribunals now grant more annulments than they did formerly does not mean that the Church has retreated from her doctrine on the unity and indissolubility of holy matrimony. The Church is guided by her Lord, who said, "They are no longer two but one. What therefore God has joined together let no man put asunder" (Mt 19:6).

36

FIDELITY IN MARRIAGE

The Sixth Commandment, which says "You shall not commit adultery" (Ex 20:14), has special reference to the fidelity that should exist between husband and wife. God established marriage as a permanent covenant of love between a man and a woman with a view to forming the special community we call a "family". When a man and a woman take each other in Christian marriage they promise to share their bodies and their whole lives in an exclusive relationship that normally results in new human life. Marriage, which was instituted by God for the propagation of the human race and for the natural and supernatural development of the marriage partners, requires that husband and wife be faithful to their promises. That is what fidelity means—being faithful to one's promises.

In the case of marriage, one is free either to enter into it or not; but if one does enter into the state of holy matrimony, then the norms for Christian marriage are not left to the whim of each individual. Since man and his or her sexuality have been created by God, this means that marriage must be entered into according to the law of God.

Adultery and fornication are repeatedly condemned in the Bible. Both terms are also used to designate, in a derogatory way, idolatry among the Israelites. Idol worship was considered to be a type of adultery since it involved infidelity to the Covenant with the Lord.

We read in Hebrews (13:4): "Marriage is to be honored by all, and marriages are to be kept undefiled, because fornicators and adulterers will come under God's judgment." One way to understand this passage is to take the generic term "fornication" in the sense of "prostitution". Thus two types of marital infidelity are condemned: with another person for hire, and with someone other than one's spouse but without pay.

In her teaching on marriage and the family, the Catholic Church has constantly stressed the need for fidelity and love between husband and wife. Marriage is not just legitimate fornication. It requires the total dedication of husband to wife and wife to husband. For the Christian, marriage goes much beyond its natural ends of friendship and procreation. Since it is a sacrament instituted by Jesus Christ to signify and confer divine grace, for those called to it it is their way to sanctification and to eternal life. For, in the plan of God, husbands and wives should help each other in the attainment of heaven and the beatific vision. If their community of life leads them into serious sin, then there is something radically wrong somewhere.

The Old Testament condemns adultery, but does not go much beyond that in the field of sexual morality. In the New Testament the Sixth Commandment is expanded to cover a multitude of sins against the virtue of chastity. Thus, Christians are warned, especially in apostolic letters, to avoid licentiousness, unnatural sexual conduct, fornication, incest and prostitution.

The Christians who lived in the Roman Empire of the first century were exposed to every imaginable kind of impurity and sexual perversion. Sexual license, much like today, enjoyed great public approval. The writers and playwrights of the time glorified infidelity, pederasty and homosexuality. The Apostles endeavored to protect their Christian converts from the contemporary sexual perversions. It is clear from Paul's words in Romans (1:24–27) that he condemned what we now call masturbation and homosexuality. Here is what Paul says:

> That is why God left them to their filthy enjoyments and the practices with which they dishonor their own bodies, since they have given up divine truth for a lie. . . . That is why God has abandoned them to degrading passions: why their women have turned from natural intercourse to unnatural practices and why their menfolk have given up natural intercourse to be consumed with passion for each other, men doing shameless things with men and getting an appropriate reward for their perversion.

The early Christians were taught by the Apostles that the practice of purity and fidelity was not just a list of do's and don'ts. It also involved the way of truth and the way of life. The sexual perversions of the pagans, both then and now, are intimately connected with grave errors both in philosophy and theology. The Christian who is "pure of heart" not only avoids sexual immorality, but he also leads a wholesome life based on truth rather than on error.

37

BLUEPRINT FOR A CHRISTIAN SOCIETY

In the contemporary world there is perhaps no teaching of the Catholic Church that is better known than that she is implacably opposed to artificial contraception. Here it is not my concern to discuss the dissent over this teaching which exists both inside and outside the Church. The point I wish to make is that the Catholic Church, in her highest authority and with the concurrence of bishops around the world, not only now but continuously and universally since the early Fathers in the second century, has taught and still teaches that any positive and direct interference with the marital act that would render it infecund, is contrary to the law of God in a serious way, and therefore is a mortal sin.

Ours is a contraceptive society and has been at least since the Lambeth Conference in 1930 when, under pressure from Margaret Sanger and the Planned Parenthood group, the Anglican bishops approved a limited form of artificial birth control. Until that time both Catholics and Protestants, though divided on many doctrinal issues for four centuries, condemned artificial contraception. Since 1930, however, most Protestant bodies have sided with the Anglicans. Among national groups of any influence in the United States the Roman Catholic Church is one of the few that has remained steadfast in her condemnation of contraception; she is joined in this position by some smaller fundamentalist religions such as the Mormons.

Andrew Greeley, the priest–sociologist–columnist, claims that this teaching, which runs counter to the trends in our culture, is the principal reason for the large number of defections from the Church during the past ten years. You can find the statistics on this in the first part of the revised draft of the *National Catechetical Directory*.

It is no secret hidden from the laity that there is a great deal of dissent among Catholic theologians at the present time with regard to certain official teachings of the Catholic Church. In fact, dissent is now so common that it is often difficult to name a well-known Catholic theologian who is not a dissenter on some point or other. Dissent, in the sense of disagreeing with official Catholic teaching, is especially prominent with regard to artificial birth control. The names of such well-known theologians as Charles Curran, Richard McCormick, S.J., Bernard Haering, Hans Küng and Joseph Fuchs, S.J., come immediately to mind.

In previous times in the Church such dissenters would have been silenced immediately. But now we live in a permissive society in which it is not fashionable to impose sanctions on dissenters. This is true not only in civil society but also in the Catholic Church. One result of this permissiveness is that many people are confused and do not know what to believe, for, on the one hand, the Church teaches officially that artificial contraception in all cases is against the law of God, and, on the other hand, respected Catholic professors openly contradict that teaching and are not rebuked or sanctioned either by the Pope or by the bishops. This situation has been tolerated for some time now, but I am of the opinion that the growing conflict between the Magisterium (teaching authority) and theologians will soon come to a head. And there is no doubt in my mind who will prevail.

A few years ago Cardinal John Wright, at the time Prefect of the Congregation for the Clergy in Rome, pointed out that there is an essential difference between faith and theology. Faith comes from God and is permanent; theology is a human creation that comes and goes. Theology can help to illuminate faith and to deepen it, but it cannot and must not replace it.

Our Lord and Savior Jesus Christ commissioned his Apostles and their successors to teach all nations with authority in his name (cf. Mt 28:18–20). He ordered them to preach the Gospel. He did not send them forth to be purveyors of theological opinions. The bishops have always used the services of theologians, but it is the bishops who teach with the authority of Christ, not theologians.

Pope Paul VI listened to theologians before he wrote his now famous letter on human life, *Humanae Vitae*. But he did not follow the recommendations of the majority nor was he under any necessity to do so. If you are concerned about the problems of human life today, I would urge you to read that letter. The letter is truly prophetic, covering most of the burning questions of the day, such as contraception, sterilization, abortion, euthanasia and so forth. The letter does much more than just declare the constant tradition of the Church that artificial contraception is contrary to the will of God and therefore immoral. It also offers a blueprint for a Christian, civilized society in which all human life is respected because it comes from God and is ordered back to God.

38

PREMARITAL SEX IS STILL FORNICATION

One characteristic of our age is the tendency to change the names of things. This practice is especially prevalent in the area of sexual morality. Thus, many now speak of "premarital relations" or "premarital sex" when they are referring to fornication. Seemingly, fornication—so often condemned in the Bible and explicitly termed a mortal sin by the Church—is a word that is too harsh for soft modern ears. "Premarital relations" sounds much better—and also, one cannot find a single passage in the Bible, not even in St. Paul, that condemns it.

But no matter what you call it, fornication still remains fornication. It is defined as voluntary sexual intercourse between unmarried persons and it has been forbidden to the followers of Christ since the beginning of Christianity. Objectively considered, it is always a mortal sin.

It is one of the sins that excludes those guilty of it from the Kingdom of God. Thus, we read in Ephesians (5:5): "For you can be quite certain that nobody who actually indulges in fornication or impurity or promiscuity —which is worshipping a false god—can inherit anything of the kingdom of God." Again in 1 Corinthians (6:18) St. Paul says: "Keep away from fornication. All the other sins are committed outside the body; but to fornicate is to sin against your own body." (See also 1 Cor 5:1; 6:9; 10:8; 1 Tim 1:10; Heb 13:4.) Jesus himself explicitly condemns fornication in Mark (7:21): "For it is from within, from men's hearts, that evil intentions emerge: fornication, theft, murder, adultery. . . ."

Premarital sex or fornication is evil because it is forbidden by the law of God. But the reason why it is forbidden by God is that it is contrary to the true good of man and woman. There is no denying the fact that sexual intercourse is by nature ordered to the procreation of children. Unless it is frustrated by the direct intervention of the man or the woman, the marital embrace, if performed at the right time and in the proper manner, will, if both parents are healthy and the woman is within the child-bearing age, in due course result in the conception of offspring.

But children need loving care in order to grow up as responsible human beings. The physical, psychological, intellectual, social and economic well being of a child requires the stability of the family. If the child is not reared by a father and a mother who truly care for him or her, then one or all of these necessary qualities will be lacking. And experience shows that men and women who do not mature in a healthy family environment often are themselves disturbed individuals who, rather

231

than contributing to society, are a burden on society. So both the good of the individual and the good of society in general require that sex and babies be confined to families—to those men and women who commit themselves to each other. Pope Paul VI stated this well in his 1968 encyclical *Humanae Vitae* (8):

> Husband and wife, through that mutual gift of themselves which is properly theirs and exclusive to them alone, develop that union of two persons in which they perfect one another, in order to cooperate with God in the generation and education of new lives.

It is no argument to maintain that now the "pill" or other contraceptives exclude the possibility of conception and that therefore fornication is allowable, at least in those cases where the partners are "committed" to each other and do not exploit each other. Aside from the fact that artificial birth control has been repeatedly condemned by the Church as immoral, it is not possible for fornicators to be committed to each other in the same way that married people are.

In December of 1975 the Holy See considered this problem in a document entitled, *Declaration on Certain Questions Concerning Sexual Ethics*. In response to the claim that those who intend to marry may legitimately engage in sexual intercourse, the Vatican declared (7):

> This opinion is contrary to Christian doctrine, which states that every genital act must be within the framework of marriage. However firm the intention of those who practice such premature sexual relations may be, the fact remains that these relations cannot ensure, in sincerity and fidelity, the interpersonal relationship between a man and a woman, nor especially can they protect this relationship from whims and caprices.

The *Declaration* goes on to show that Jesus willed a stable union between a man and a woman in indissoluble marriage. Then it states:

> Sexual union therefore is only legitimate if a definitive community of life has been established between the man and the woman. This is what the Church has always understood and taught, and she finds a profound agreement with her doctrine in men's reflection and in the lessons of history.

Finally, those Catholics today who argue for the legitimacy of fornication in certain circumstances must distort the obvious meaning of the Bible, must ignore the constant tradition of the Church, and must reject the clear, current teaching of our Holy Mother, the Church.

39

CATHOLIC VIEW OF HOMOSEXUALITY

In the past few chapters we have explored the teaching of the Church in some of the most important areas covered by the Sixth Commandment—both what the Commandment postively enjoins on the believing Christian and what it forbids.

In this essay I would like to take up briefly the delicate matter of homosexuality. I use the word "delicate" advisedly, for when I was growing up and attending high school in the 1940s the subject was rarely mentioned in any public utterance, was banned in movies and on the radio, and was usually referred to only in hushed tones even by young boys on the street. Now that is all changed. Homosexuality is such a common topic not only in conversation but also in the media, in movies, on television and in politics, that it is necessary to write about it openly in Catholic newspapers.

According to the *New Catholic Encyclopedia* (volume 6), a homosexual or invert is "anyone who is erotically attracted to a notable degree toward persons of his or her own sex and who engages, or is psychologically disposed to engage, in sexual activity prompted by this attraction." In popular conversation usually no distinction is drawn between the psychological inclination to homosexuality and its actual expression, although it is important to keep this in mind since there is a very important difference between the two realities.

It is not my concern here to discuss the problem of the responsibility for the homosexual condition. An individual may or may not be personally responsible for the inclination. What we are concerned about here is the objective morality of homosexuality.

It is well known that the Catholic Church teaches that homosexuality is a perversion of the sex faculty and that therefore it is seriously wrong. In fact, the "gay" activists of our day have made it a point to zero in on the Catholic bishops as special targets, since the Catholic Church, at least up until the present time, in its official teaching, has remained adamant in its condemnation of all forms of homosexuality. One professional gay activist that I debated with on television accused the Catholic hierarchy of being "the greatest persecutors of homosexuals in the history of the world".

The basic argument used by Catholic moralists, apart from the Biblical argument, runs as follows: The sexual faculty was created by God for the transmission of human life. All sexual activity must remain open to the transmission of human life. Therefore the genital expression of sexuality must be restricted to that between man and woman, and then only in the stable relationship of marriage and the family where the children can be adequately provided for.

By its very nature the homosexual act excludes all possibility of the transmission of life. It cannot fulfill the procreative purpose of the sexual faculty and is therefore an inordinate use of that faculty. Since homosexuality runs contrary to a basic human good, it is a serious transgression of the divine will and so gravely sinful.

Homosexuality is often condemned in the Bible. The most important passages are: Genesis 19:4–11; Leviticus 18:22; 20:13; Romans 1:26–27; 1 Corinthians 6:9–10; 1 Timothy 1:9–10. For at least the past thousand years there have been numerous condemnations of the sin of homosexuality by the Roman pontiffs. The most recent was in December 1975 in the Vatican *Declaration on Certain Questions Concerning Sexual Ethics*. The *Declaration* observes that some people today are trying to justify homosexuality. "This they do in opposition to the constant teaching of the Magisterium and to the moral sense of the Christian people" (8). The document goes on to urge compassion in dealing with homosexuals but not to condone their conduct.

> For according to the objective moral order, homosexual relations are acts which lack an essential and indispensable finality. In Sacred Scriptures they are condemned as a serious depravity

and even presented as the sad consequence of rejecting God. This judgment of Scripture does not of course permit us to conclude that all those who suffer from this anomaly are personally responsible for it, but it does attest to the fact that homosexual acts are intrinsically disordered and can in no case be approved of.

That is the official teaching of the Catholic Church —and it is not going to change. True, there are some so-called "Catholic" moralists who today are demanding that the Church approve of homosexual "marriages". They get much space in the press and time on television talk shows. But do not be deceived by them. What some Catholic intellectuals or "moralists" say on television is not necessarily what the Catholic Church teaches. In the present age of permissiveness and confusion it is not difficult to find some "Catholic professor" who will deny any and all traditional Catholic teachings.

In order to keep your bearings in the present fog, it is necessary to hold on to Peter and his successor, our Holy Father.

40

WHAT IS AND WHAT SHOULD BE

It is not easy to write clearly and adequately about such a delicate, personal and private moral matter as masturbation. But I have set myself the task of covering the basics of the Ten Commandments. Within the area of the Sixth Commandment there are two subjects yet to cover—masturbation and pornography. Now I will treat the former, and in the following essay I will treat the latter. I feel that I would be failing in thoroughness if I passed this matter over in silence.

We all know what masturbation or self-abuse is, but perhaps we cannot all define it. Moralists define it as complete sexual satisfaction obtained by some form of self-stimulation. As a result of studies made during the past thirty years, especially by Dr. A. C. Kinsey and his collaborators, we know that masturbation is very common among young males at or after puberty, and fairly common among girls and women. This comes as no surprise to experienced confessors who have spent thousands of hours administering the Sacrament of Penance or Reconciliation.

The constant and clear teaching of the Catholic Church, based on principles found in Holy Scripture, is that deliberately procured masturbation is a mortal sin—one that excludes from the kingdom of God (cf. 1 Cor 6:9–10). In assigning a reason for such a serious prohibition, the Church teaches that sexual activity is meant by God its Creator to foster the propagation of the human race and the mutual love of man and woman in the stable union of holy matrimony. In fact, sex in marriage, far from leading away from God, can and should be a means for the sanctification of both marriage partners.

The traditional Catholic teaching that deliberate masturbation constitutes a grave moral disorder is often challenged or even denied in contemporary American society. It is stated that modern psychology and sociology have shown that masturbation in young people and in single men and women is both common and natural. It is further asserted that self-abuse involves no moral fault, unless it is the result of some anti-social behavior that somehow denies the personal worth of others. One well-known "Catholic" theologian at a major Catholic university publicly ridiculed the 1975 papal *Declaration on Certain Questions Concerning Sexual Ethics* for stating that masturbation "is an intrinsically and seriously disordered act". In his view self-abuse is no different morally than eating and drinking and he recommended dropping it completely from the field of serious moral discourse.

Such a view may be shocking but it is not uncommon among some contemporary "Catholic" theologians. For example, in 1977 the Catholic Theological Society of America (CTSA) published a book, *Human Sexuality*, which was written by a five person committee of the same society. The book takes a very permissive view of masturbation, homosexuality, fornication, adultery and other sexual vices. In this case, fortunately, there was a strong reaction and rejection from such quarters as Archbishop John Quinn of San Francisco, Cardinal William Baum of Washington and Professor William E. May of the Catholic University of America.

Please be clear on the following point. When I restate the Church's constant condemnation of masturbation, I am not passing any judgment on the subjective guilt of those who masturbate. Responsibility in this matter is very complex and difficult to pinpoint. Sexual emission may be voluntary or involuntary; it can occur while sleeping or awake; due to ignorance or false instruction many youths may not know that self-abuse is wrong,

238

and so forth. What we are talking about here is the *objective* morality of masturbation.

The Magisterium of the Church has been and is very clear in stating that

> masturbation is an intrinsically and seriously disordered act. The main reason is that, whatever the motive for acting this way, the deliberate use of the sexual faculty outside normal conjugal relations essentially contradicts the finality of this faculty. For it lacks the sexual relationship called for by the moral order, namely the relationship which realizes 'the full sense of mutual self-giving and human procreation in the context of true love.' All deliberate exercise of sexuality must be reserved to this regular relationship (1975 *Declaration*, 9).

And even though masturbation is a common human failure—as a result of original sin and a corrupted environment—the *Declaration* clearly rejects the popular notion that sociological surveys on the frequency of this sin can be used to "constitute a criterion for judging the moral value of human acts." That is, just because it is frequent does not mean that it is morally good. For, if frequency alone of a human act were the criterion of its morality, then, since most people lie at least some times, one would have to conclude that lying is natural and therefore good and holy. We should always remember that there is a very important difference between *what is* and *what should be*. Sociology may tell us what is. Divine revelation and its only authentic interpreter, the holy Roman Catholic Church, tell us what should be in matters of faith and morals.

41

PORNOGRAPHY AND
THE NINTH COMMANDMENT

So far we have covered, for the most part, the more common and important *external* sins against the Sixth Commandment. But there is more to Christian sexual morality than just avoiding adultery, fornication and other sexual sins. There is also the matter of purity of heart. Jesus made many improvements on the Jewish understanding of the law of God. One of the most important was his stress on the fact that morality, for the Christian, must reach beyond the external deed and embrace the heart. Right at the beginning of his famous Sermon on the Mount, in the sixth beatitude, he said: "Blessed are the pure of heart for they shall see God" (Mt 5:8). True, "purity of heart" in this verse includes much more than just sexual purity, but it certainly does include that also.

Adultery, as we have seen, is forbidden explicitly by the Sixth Commandment. But there is also the Ninth Commandment which remains to be considered in connection with the Sixth. The Ninth Commandment says: "You shall not covet your neighbor's wife" (Dt 5:21). This means that the law of God forbids, not just the physical act of adultery, but also the interior, mental desire or plan to do so. Jesus was also explicit on this point when he said in the same Sermon on the Mount: "You have learned how it was said: You must not commit adultery. But I say this to you: if a man looks at a woman lustfully, he has already committed adultery with her in his heart" (Mt 5:27–28).

It has been the constant teaching of the Church, therefore, that impure or unchaste thoughts and desires are to be carefully avoided. Sometimes, it is true, such thoughts and desires afflict men and women of all ages, beginning around the age of puberty and lasting until the moment of death. Such thoughts and desires, though contrary to the Ninth Commandment of God, are sinful only when and to the extent that they are *deliberate*. For, a human being is not held accountable by God for thoughts or actions that do not proceed from full knowledge and full consent of the will. Confessors and spiritual directors can offer much helpful advice on how to handle these problems.

The divine prohibition against "lustful thoughts and looks" immediately brings to mind the present flood of pornography in newspapers, magazines, books, films and, increasingly, in television and radio. As we know from regular reports about court cases concerning the subject, pornography is not easy to define. I will use the definition offered by Mr. Malcolm Muggeridge (*Pornography: The Longford Report*, Wm. B. Eerdmans, 1977, p. 412).

> For our purposes, the general characteristics of pornography may be taken as being the use of eroticism for ulterior purposes. It embraces, on the one hand, violence and sexual perversion, and on the other, smuttiness and obscenity. Most often commercial motives are present.

Common to all pornography is that it portrays or describes explicit sexual material—very often of a perverted kind; the purpose is to stimulate sexual desire and pleasure, usually leading to masturbation; it is produced for commercial exploitation; and it presents sex in a degrading and dehumanizing way that is offensive to Christian and ordinary human decency.

Evidence is mounting each month that pornography is the cause of many social evils in our society. However, that is not our concern here. The point I want to make is that one of the main purposes of pornographic materials is to arouse passion, to stimulate sexual desire, to seek immediate gratification in sexual pleasure. From the point of view of Catholic morality, all such deliberate desires outside of marriage are contrary to God's Ninth Commandment in a serious way and therefore mortal sins.

Man cannot violate one of God's laws for long with impunity. We see this in the matters of lying, contraception, abortion, stealing, denial of basic human rights, and so forth. We see it also in the vile traffic in pornography. And we are not just talking about children, since the purpose of pornography is to stimulate "lustful thoughts and desires" which are forbidden by God to adults as well as to children.

Lest there be any misunderstanding about the intent of porn, let me conclude by quoting the Englishman, Steven Marcus, author of *The Other Victorians*:

> Literature possesses a multitude of intentions but pornography possesses only one . . . its aim is to move us in the direction of action. Pornography is obsessed with the idea of pleasure, of infinite pleasure, the idea of gratification.

42

ATTENTION ALL THIEVES AND MUGGERS

The plan of these essays has been to explain the basics of
the Ten Commandments. Having covered most of the
present crucial areas of the Sixth and Ninth Commandments, we will now move on to the Seventh and Tenth.
Because of the tremendous complexities of our modern
economy and also because of the worldwide struggle
between capitalism and communism, it will not be possible in this space to treat all of the problems nor even
to treat the topics chosen in a detailed or exhaustive
manner. What I propose to do is to give the Church's
teaching on the most basic and fundamental questions
that arise in the area of the rights of ownership of
property and their violation.

The biblical injunction against theft is clear and un-
ambiguous: "You shall not steal" (Ex 20:15; Dt 5:19).
This is followed up with a prohibition against coveting
or desiring or setting one's heart on another's property:
"You shall not covet your neighbor's . . . servant, man
or woman, or his ox, or his donkey, or anything that is
his" (Ex 20:17; Dt 5:21).

Going beyond this general law, the Old Testament
also forbids robbery, usury, fraud and the deliberate
destruction of other people's property. There are special
precepts that deal with changing boundary markers,
false weights and measures and profiteering on hired
help.

In order to make sure that the laws against theft were observed, the Mosaic law prescribed severe sanctions on those who were guilty of violating them. As a general rule, the thief was held to restore twice the value of what he had stolen in order to be forgiven. In the case of some animals, he had to restore four or five for each one stolen. Thus, there is no doubt that stealing was held to be a very serious offense against the Lord in the Old Testament. The prophets frequently denounced stealing —both that of individual against individual and especially that practiced by the rich and powerful against the poor. Such passages are rather frequent in Amos and Jeremiah.

Jesus, followed by his faithful Apostles, especially Sts. Peter and Paul, repeated the Mosaic denunciation of thievery. For example, when the rich young man asked him what he should do to attain eternal life, our Savior told him to keep the Commandments, quoting, among others, the Seventh Commandment: "You must not steal" (Mk 10:19). St. Paul told those who were thieves and crooks before their conversion to change their ways: "Anyone who was a thief must stop stealing; he should try to find some useful manual work instead, and be able to do some good by helping others that are in need" (Eph 4:28).

What do we mean by stealing? Catholic moralists define stealing as the deliberate taking of something against the reasonable will of its owner. To steal secretly is called "theft", while using or threatening violence in the act of taking is called "robbery". Thus, mugging is a type of robbery; cheating, keeping found articles whose owners could easily be discovered, neglecting to pay one's debts, are considered equivalent to theft.

Theft and robbery are contrary to the natural law of God and are opposed to *justice*, which requires that we give to each one his due. The fact that God's law forbids stealing is an implicit affirmation of the right to the private ownership of property that belongs to others. For, if there were no right of ownership, then everything would belong to everybody and there could be no such thing as stealing: everyone could help himself at any time to whatever he wanted. Obviously, such a situation would result in chaos and would be the end of any type of peaceful social life.

Theft and robbery are mortal sins, unless that which is stolen is of little value. But even if the amount taken is only a few dollars, the violence involved in a robbery or a mugging may make it a mortal sin. It is often very difficult to distinguish between light and grave matters, that is, between what would be sufficient matter for a venial sin or a mortal sin. Due to varying standards of living this will vary from country to country, and even in the same country from region to region.

43

IS STEALING EVER A MORTAL SIN?

Stealing is not as uncommon as many people seem to think it is. Each year thefts from shops, supermarkets and department stores run into the hundreds of millions of dollars. It takes a great number of individuals to steal a hundred million dollars worth of food from supermarkets. And look at our cities. In New York City anything of value left out in the open unprotected for just a few minutes will infallibly be stolen. This does not include the two hundred cars stolen each day, the break-ins and numerous daily muggings. The situation is vividly described simply by recalling the famous garbage strike in the early 1970s: one creative New Yorker wrapped his garbage in an attractive box and left it on the seat of his car each day while at work. The car doors being locked, the garbage was taken every day by some unsuspecting thief. That may be a good way to dispose of garbage but it is not very complimentary to the citizenry.

Stealing has become a way of life for many Americans. There are several reasons for this, some of which include the need for addictive drugs such as alcohol and heroin, a perverted understanding, coming from Marxist ideology, of the individual's right to his own property, and the laxity of our courts in dealing with thieves. But just because thievery is common and treated leniently by the police and the courts, it does not follow that it is not a serious sin. One of the reasons for the breakdown of order in our society is that too many people do not respect the property of others.

A question often asked priests, and one that is not easy to answer, concerns the amount of stolen goods necessary to constitute a venial sin or a mortal sin. I will try to answer this question on the basis of traditional Catholic moral teaching. Let me say that it is tempting just to avoid this matter, but the consciences of many people are uneasy here and they want some sort of guidelines.

Because of this uneasiness and questioning, moralists are forced to draw some lines.

First of all, to steal something of small value is wrong but it is not a mortal sin. What is meant by "small value"? Well, in general, it would include ordinary items that would cost less than a few dollars. Some examples might be: a newspaper, a magazine, a candy bar, a package of cigarettes, a pound of butter, a pair of stockings, and so forth. However, moralists hasten to add that if a person steals small amounts of money or goods over a period of time with the intention of *accumulating* a large amount, the small thefts would "coalesce" into the grave matter required for a mortal sin.

In evaluating the matter necessary for a mortal sin of theft it is necessary to distinguish between what is "relatively grave matter" and what is "absolutely grave matter". This distinction of the moralists is based on the objective fact that what is of little value in itself may be very important to a poor person, while an object of great value, say an expensive car, may not mean much to a wealthy person.

Thus, an object is said to have relatively great value, not from its own intrinsic worth, but in reference to the condition of the owner and the injury suffered. Accordingly, in order to come down to specifics, to steal a day's salary or its equivalent from a workingman would constitute relatively grave matter and would be a mortal sin. This would be true even if the amount were only twenty or thirty dollars.

"Absolutely grave matter" refers to the intrinsic value of what is stolen. A few examples will illustrate the principle: a house, five acres of land, an automobile, a good television set, a diamond ring. How much *money* would constitute "absolutely grave matter"? Up until about fifteen years ago, moralists said one hundred dollars. On the basis of continuing inflation and the decline in the value of the dollar, I think it would be safe to say that today the theft of two hundred dollars is sufficient matter, objectively and no matter whom it is taken from—whether from a millionaire or from a large corporation—to constitute "absolutely grave matter" in the area of stealing.

Moralists reason that, even though a theft of two hundred dollars or more may not impose a hardship on the owner or owners (such as a large corporation), nevertheless such a theft is a serious attack on society itself and on the public peace of the community. Such dishonesty, if unchecked, would soon lead to a serious breakdown of social order. And dishonesty which seriously disturbs the public order is always a mortal sin, because man is by nature a social being and can achieve his human perfection only in society. Thus, to steal two hundred dollars or more is always seriously sinful. However, it should be noted that the amount that constitutes absolutely grave matter in theft or robbery varies from country to country, because of different standards of living.

44

BALANCING THE SCALES OF JUSTICE

We have seen that stealing is explicitly forbidden by the Seventh Commandment. In our society theft is such a common moral failing that the amount of property stolen each year runs into billions of dollars. Stealing is a sin—venial or mortal depending on the amount stolen and the particular circumstances. But what is a person required to do who has stolen property from another and repents of his sin and asks for forgiveness in the Sacrament of Penance or Reconciliation?

The constant teaching of the Church on this point is that one who has stolen the property of another, such as a radio, television set, camera, battery, and so forth, and one who has inflicted unjust damage on another, such as deliberately damaging his car, is bound to *restitution* before he or she can be fully forgiven. The word comes from the Latin *restituere* which means "to restore something", "to set it up where it had been". Restitution then is the repairing of an injury, the righting of a wrong.

So in the eyes of God and the Church it is not sufficient for forgiveness that the thief repent of his sins; in order to demonstrate that he is truly repentant he must also give back what he has unjustly taken from a fellow human being. It amazes me that so many apparently well-educated and certainly well-meaning Catholics do not seem to know about the obligation to restitution. The obligation itself is based on the natural law. Since ownership is a true right of persons, if one is deprived by theft or unjust damage of what is his, then the taken goods must be restored to him to balance the scales of justice. To deny that there is any moral obligation to restitution is equivalent to denying the right of private property.

Further, the injustice involved in theft and unjust damage continues until it is repaired. In the Old Testament we find some very specific directives with regard to restitution, as for example in Exodus (21:37): "When a man steals an ox or a sheep and slaughters or sells it, he shall restore five oxen for the one ox, and four sheep for the one sheep."

As a general rule, restitution should be made to the injured person, or to his heirs if he is no longer living, and it should be done as soon as is morally possible. For, the injustice continues until the wrong has been righted. It is not necessary to make the restitution openly or in a way that would reveal the identity of the offending party. It can be made secretly or anonymously. For example, an employee can make restitution to his employer by doing extra work for which he is not paid.

How can restitution be made to someone whose identity is not known? Catholic moralists suggest giving the money or the goods to the poor, or to some worthy charity, or to the missions, since it can reasonably be presumed that that would be in accordance with the wishes of the injured party.

Often people are excused from restitution because of physical or moral impossibility. It is "physical" when it just cannot be done; it is "moral" when it would cause a grave hardship—a hardship worse than that inflicted on the injured party. But when the impossibility ceases, then the restitution must still be made as soon as possible. One may also be excused from restitution if the one offended forgives the debt.

The obligation to restitution is a serious moral duty which should not be brushed off lightly. In fact, it is so serious that it also extends to all those who assist another to steal property from a third party. Thus, those who urge or counsel others to steal can be held to restitution; also those whose duty it is to prevent stealing, such as policemen, watchmen and employees of various kinds, when they help others steal by turning the other way can be held to restitution.

I do not want to give the impression in this essay that restitution is a simple matter. It is not. It is a highly complex subject in Catholic moral theology. In difficult questions there are probably very few priests who can give good advice immediately in the confessional, without first consulting books on the subject or some qualified moral theologian. If the question ever comes up for you, try to find an experienced, prudent and learned priest who can help you out. Even he may ask you to wait for an answer to your question so that he can consult the experts.

45

THE RIGHT TO PRIVATE PROPERTY

The right to private property, or the right to ownership, has always been defended by the Catholic Church, from the time of the Apostles right down to Pope Paul VI. With the growing influence and threat of international communism, which denies any right to private property, it is well to consider the basis of the Catholic position.

As a human right, the right to property or ownership is the moral power that a person has to dispose of a thing and its utility according to his own free will, unless he is otherwise hindered because of the rights of others. This natural right is rooted in man's free, intellectual nature which was created by God and is constantly held in existence by him. Only persons endowed by God with intelligence and free will, have rights, such as the right to private property, in the true sense. Thus animals, since they are not rational beings, do not have moral rights. This does not mean, however, that there are no limits on how man may dispose of them. Also, a person can have true ownership of animals, but animals cannot "own" anything. Because of the intrinsic dignity of persons, they cannot be the object of ownership; for this reason slavery in all its forms is to be utterly rejected and condemned.

As a free person in this material world, man needs material possessions or property in order to achieve his full freedom and development. Please note the close connection between private property and freedom. Generally speaking, the more property a person possesses the more free he is—free in the sense of making his own decisions that concern his own life and the lives of his wife and children. On the other hand, the man who does not own anything is at the mercy of the welfare state and the whim of big time and petty bureaucrats.

That private property promotes freedom is obvious in many areas of human experience. Let us look briefly at two of them—housing and education. The person who owns property is free to live wherever he is able to buy or rent a home or an apartment. He does not have to wait ten or fifteen years to be assigned a place to live in, all at the good pleasure of the state, as is the case in Soviet Russia. His private property enables him to live where he chooses, within his means.

Freedom of education is an important dimension of full family living. The destitute person is completely at the mercy of the state—whether his children receive any education at all and what kind of education they receive. Persons of means, if they do not like what is offered in the public or state schools, can band together and provide the type of education they want for their children; freedom to act in this way presupposes the private ownership of property.

As should be clear from the above, the right to private property places a very concrete limitation on the power of the state to control the lives of its citizens. Thus, one of the main reasons why Americans enjoy so much freedom, and Russians so little, is that the Constitution of the United States recognizes the inherent right to private property while the Soviet Union does not.

That every person has a right to private ownership of property can also be shown from the Bible. For, in the Seventh Commandment the Lord forbids theft. This serious prohibition would be meaningless unless ownership were a prior and natural right given to man when he was first created by God. Respect for the property of others is inculcated by the Bible from beginning to end.

It is good to reflect on man's natural right to property in these days of rapidly rising taxes (which, if uncontrolled can in effect deny that right), of the spread of communism and communist ideas on the nature of property, of misrepresentation of the Church's true teaching by an erroneous explanation of "social justice". Social justice in Catholic teaching is a difficult and complex concept. We must be alert to the current attempts of idealogues, both Catholic and materialist, to promote the communist idea of property under the guise of the Catholic teaching about social justice.

The true Catholic teaching about the right to private property is expounded lucidly in modern times in the social encyclicals of Popes Leo XIII and Pius XI. The doctrine is clear for those who have eyes to see, but in the present dangerous climate I would like to see our Holy Father come out once again with a significant document explaining and affirming the personal right to private property.

46

BOTH CHARITY AND JUSTICE

In a previous essay I have shown that each human person has a natural right to private property. This right extends not only to personal goods such as a home, clothing, jewelry, an automobile, and so forth, but it also embraces productive property such as farms, factories and businesses of all kinds. There is no question that this is the teaching of the Catholic Church and that this teaching is true. But we must be careful in the defense of private property that we do not try to prove too much. For, as they used to say when I studied logic, "He who proves too much proves nothing."

The point I want to stress here is that the right to private property is not an absolute right, that is, it is limited and conditioned by a number of other factors. There are two extremes in this matter—and both of them must be avoided if we are to find the truth. One view holds that the right to private property is absolute, in the sense that the lawful owner can do anything he wishes with his possessions since they belong to him. This is a form of "rugged individualism" which has been denounced in Catholic social teaching because it wholly ignores, and implicitly denies, the social nature of man. The teaching of the Bible and of the Fathers and of the popes bears witness to the fact that "the world is given to all, and not only to the rich" (St. Ambrose).

The other extreme simply denies that man has a natural right to private ownership. This is the view of the communists and various types of socialists, social reformers, anarchists and utopians. For the latter types, all ownership resides in the state. Since the goods of the earth are meant for everyone, according to the communists the state is the only agency (theoretically) that can guarantee an equal distribution of those goods to all the citizens. This sounds plausible in theory and was devised as a means to eliminate from human history the cruelty and oppression that has often been exercised by the wealthy in the past. In a word, it is an effort to cut down the rich and raise up the poor. But just because some rich people have abused their property it does not follow that the right to private property should be lost or denied. Just because some people drive recklessly and kill others it does not follow that all cars should be destroyed.

Catholic social teaching insists that the right of property is distinct from its use. Commutative justice, that is, the justice that governs the proper relations between individuals, demands that each individual respect the property of others; otherwise the Seventh and Tenth Commandments would not make much sense. However, there are also moral norms that bind property owners. In addition to respecting the strict rights of others, since the goods of the earth were created by God for all mankind, there are times when property owners must place at least some of their possessions at the disposal of the community or the common good. Thus, if the common good requires it, a property owner may be forced out of his house in order to make way for a new highway. Also, a person in extreme necessity, that is, dying from hunger, may licitly take fruit from the orchard of another in order to sustain his life. The reasoning here is that one person's right to his own life takes precedence over the right of another to his superfluous goods. Admittedly, this principle can be abused by the unscrupulous, but nevertheless the principle stands as correct.

Here is what Vatican II had to say on this matter: "God intended the earth and all it contains for the use of all men and peoples, so created goods should flow fairly to all, regulated by justice and accompanied by charity" (*The Church in the Modern World*, 69).

Strict justice, which means giving to each person what is his due or what is coming to him, must certainly be observed by all in the matter of private property. But there is more to this serious problem than justice. There is also a question of charity. All are bound by charity also, and one can be bound in charity to help another even though it is not a question of strict justice. Thus both charity and justice go together in solving social problems and working for the common good. The harmonious combination of both charity and justice in working towards a just social order in the modern world is what the popes mean by "social justice".

47

A FAIR DAY'S WORK
FOR A FAIR DAY'S PAY

A vast and complicated area of human relationships that comes under the heading of the Seventh Commandment is that of labor and management. Since all men are held morally to act justly with regard to their own possessions and the possessions of others, the labor contract, as a free human act, is governed by God's law just as all human acts are. The labor contract involves two parties—labor and management. Therefore both parties are obliged to act justly in their dealings with each other.

The Church has had much to say about the reciprocal relations between labor and management. Some of the major papal documents which touch on this subject are *Rerum Novarum* of Leo XIII, *Quadragesimo Anno* of Pius XI, *Mater et Magistra* of John XXIII and *Populorum Progressio* of Paul VI. Vatican Council II also had much to say about this subject in its *The Church in the Modern World*.

Church teaching in this field has not attempted to tell labor and management what to do in specific cases. That is not the role of the Church and, indeed, the Church is just not competent in this area. What the Church has done is to explicate the principles of justice, as known from the nature of man and from divine revelation, that should govern contracts, wages, working conditions, etc. between labor and management.

What the Church has done in her social teaching is to stress the fact that both labor and management or capital have rights which must be respected by the other party. For example, this meant in the nineteenth century that the Church supported the right of workers to organize into unions in order to be able to bargain more effectively with management for better wages. At the time it was necessary to stress the rights of workers to organize since many huge industrial interests were trying to stop the labor movement. In our day, in some areas of the economy, the shoe is on the other foot; that is to say, some unions have become much more powerful than the companies they work for and often force at least the smaller concerns to close because they cannot meet the exorbitant demands of labor. I for one think it is about time that the Church speak out forcefully on the rights of capital and management, reminding big labor that it does not have the right to run roughshod over the small proprietor.

The principal weapon or lever of labor is the strike. As a general rule, strikes hurt both labor and management and should be used only as a last resort. Catholic moralists hold that in disputes labor should first attempt reasonable bargaining with management before resorting to a strike. So, strikes must be conducted in a just and orderly manner, avoiding all use of violence or threats of violence.

A just labor contract imposes obligations on both labor and management. Christian workers need to be reminded that they have a moral obligation to give a fair day's work for a fair day's pay. Deliberately to loaf and sleep on the job is a type of stealing, since the worker has contracted to do a certain type of work for a definite wage.

Employers, on the other hand, are obliged to pay a just wage. To determine precisely in every situation what a "just wage" is can be extremely difficult. For a workingman with a family, it means an income that is sufficient to meet the ordinary needs of himself, his wife and his children. Normally, unions play a very important role in securing adequate pay for their members.

As we pointed out before in speaking of social justice, the Christian concept of man requires that in the social order justice be tempered with charity, that is, with love of God and love of one's fellow men. This applies in a very special way to the labor contract. In the Catholic view, labor and management are partners in the same enterprise, namely, to produce the goods and services necessary for a full human life—a life in which all can attain human maturity and work out their eternal salvation. Therefore they should work together.

Finally, let us recall that the Church has a lofty notion of work, since work ennobles a man's character and makes him more like Jesus who worked most of his earthly life. Here is what Vatican II says about work (*The Church in the Modern World*, 67):

> Whether done independently or managed by others, work proceeds directly from a person, who puts his seal on the things of nature and submits them to his will. By his work, man normally maintains his life and the lives of those dependent on him, is united with his fellow men and serves them, can exercise charity to the full and associate himself with perfecting the divine creation. Indeed, we hold that by his labor, man is associated with the redemptive work of Christ, who conferred surpassing dignity on labor by working with his own hands at Nazareth. Hence arises an obligation for each to work loyally, and also a right to work.

48

THE THRILL OF GAMBLING

A final consideration in the vast area of the Seventh and Tenth Commandments is the question of betting and gambling. Gambling is on the increase in this country. Las Vegas is doing a booming business; more states are sponsoring lotteries in order to raise money for an ailing school system; Atlantic City hopes to rival Las Vegas as the gambling capital of the country.

Let us begin by giving a definition. Gambling is the staking of money or other valuables on some fact or the outcome of some event that is unknown or uncertain to the participants. Betting on horses is one of the most common forms of gambling. Because of the uncertainty of the outcome, games of all types—football, baseball, basketball—are the occasion of betting. The essential feature in all gambling is the act of wagering or hazarding as such. Almost any future, contingent event lends itself as a possible object of a wager, as, for example, how much rain will fall in the month of June, the exact second when the ice on the Yukon River will break up, and so forth.

Gambling is not a modern invention. It has a long history, stretching back to Greece and Rome; it has flourished in China for untold centuries. In ancient and modern times gambling has had both its supporters and its opponents.

Why do people gamble? Perhaps the simplest answer is because they enjoy the thrill of it. There is a certain excitement associated with a wager on a horse or a football game or a throw of the dice. Betting distracts many people from the drab routine of everyday living.

Many social evils can flow from immoderate gambling. It is for this reason that most countries, and most states in the U.S.A., have strict laws governing the whole field of betting and gambling. When gambling becomes an addiction it can lead to all kinds of evils, such as stealing, robbery, lying, neglect of duty, drunkenness and suicide. Some religious bodies oppose all gambling as essentially evil since, they say, it turns a man away from trust in divine providence and from faith in God to a vain confidence in "luck" and "good fortune".

The Catholic Church has never condemned gambling as evil, although moralists have constantly warned the faithful about the dangers of immoderate gambling. The basic reason why moderate gambling is not illicit is that a person is entitled to dispose of his own property as he wills, provided that he does not render himself incapable of fulfilling his other duties, such as caring for his family and paying his debts.

Thus gambling can be sinful when a person has no right to risk the money he bets, either because it does not belong to him or because he needs it to fulfill other obligations. Gambling can be sinful for certain types of persons who know from past experience that they lose control of themselves and are in danger of squandering all their resources, to the detriment of themselves and their family.

Moreover, it is immoral to bet on a certain thing, unless the other party has been warned and still insists on betting. Thus, it would be immoral to bet on a game that is being replayed on television, when one party knows the outcome and the other does not know it is a replay. Of course, all forms of fraud and deceit must be avoided in betting.

Lotteries are a rather special case, since the chance of winning is so small. It is generally understood that the lotteries sponsored by religious and charitable organizations, as well as those run by the state, return only a portion of the income to the winners, with the surplus going to some good cause. Those who buy chances in such lotteries are either implicitly or explicitly making a contribution to the good cause, with a small chance of winning something in return.

One form of gambling that is especially dear to Catholics is *bingo*, which is a type of lottery. For years a high percentage of Catholic parochial schools have been kept in existence by means of the weekly bingo game—which is not only small scale gambling but is also an important social event for many elderly people who do not otherwise get out of their homes.

In conclusion, it is important to remember that gambling is licit, provided that one can do so without neglecting other obligations. Moderation here is essential. If a person cannot control his "urge to bet" once he gets started, then he should not bet at all.

49

OUR DEBT OF TRUTH

Having considered the goods of property, it now remains to see what God says about the goods of the mind and social communication between men and women. This whole matter is covered succinctly by the Eighth Commandment which declares: "You shall not bear false witness against your neighbor" (Ex 20:16; Dt 5:20).

In its most obvious meaning the Commandment forbids any type of lying, no matter what the circumstances and no matter what the cost to the person or persons involved. In the Old Testament lying is considered an abomination. Listen to what the book of Proverbs has to say: "Lips that tell the truth abide firm forever, the tongue that lies lasts only for a moment. Lips that lie are abhorrent to Yahweh; dear to him those who speak the truth" (12:19, 22). A similar condemnation of lying is expressed in the book of Sirach: "Lying is an ugly blot on a man, and ever on the lips of the ignorant. A thief is preferable to an inveterate liar, but both are heading for ruin. Lying is an abominable habit, so that disgrace is the liar's forever" (20:24–28).

The New Testament, of course, repeats the Eighth Commandment, as enunciated in the Old Law, but now the motivation has been changed. The Christian should avoid all unrighteousness and all falsehood because he is a new creature in Christ Jesus. St. Paul summarizes this notion clearly in Ephesians (4:24–25): "Therefore, putting away falsehood, let every one speak the truth with his neighbor." The strongest words in the New

Testament about telling the truth are found in the letter of St. James, the Apostle, who says, "The only man who could reach perfection would be someone who would never say anything wrong—he would be able to control every part of himself" (James 3:12). In the same chapter St. James points out that control of the tongue is an outward sign that the Christian has achieved complete mastery over his mind and his heart.

Since the time of the early Fathers of the Church, lying has been minutely analyzed by countless theologians and saints. The basic component of a lie is that someone deliberately says or communicates something that is contrary to what he or she thinks. Thus, if someone asks me, "Did you go to Mass yesterday," and I reply, "Yes, I did," when in fact I did not, that is a lie. For, it is a communication of something which is contrary to what I know to be a fact or to be true.

A lie is contrary to the truth. But what is truth? Truth is fundamentally a relationship of conformity between what is in the mind and reality that exists outside the mind. If the relationship is viewed from the thing to the intellect so that the intellect is formed according to reality, then it is called logical truth. In a moral sense, truth exists where there is conformity between what one thinks and what one says to others with the intention of communicating something. Truth in the moral sense is subject to the control of the human will. Since that conformity can be distorted in a number of different ways, the will needs to be trained and habituated to expressing only what it knows to be true. Such a habit is known as the virtue of truthfulness.

The virtue of truthfulness is supremely important for the happiness of the individual and the good of human society, for it keeps the human mind in touch with external reality and it avoids all deceit, and all the evils which follow upon deceit, in human relationships. By being truthful a person is and becomes good in the moral order, because he finds his own fulfillment in being faithful to the reality that is outside of himself or transcends him.

It is a truism of philosophy that lying breaks down human relationships and is destructive of human society. When a husband and wife regularly lie to each other, there can be no communion of life between them. When a government lies to its people, the people learn to distrust everything that government does. Communism and the Communist party are founded on lies and deceit; that is not a slanderous statement since they openly declare that promises, treaties and contracts are only intermediate means to attain the ultimate end—the domination of the Communist party. Since lies are humanly destructive, therefore, in the long run communism will destroy itself. Truthfulness, on the other hand, leads to human fulfillment, justice and peace. St. Thomas Aquinas said that the truth is something that we owe to others—like a debt to be paid. Thus he wrote (*Summa Theologica*, II–II, q. 109, art. 3, ad 1):

> Since man is a social animal, one man naturally owes another whatever is necessary for the preservation of human society. Now it would be impossible for men to live together, unless they believed one another, as declaring the truth one to another. Hence the virtue of truth does in some sense regard the truth as something owed.

50

LYING AND MENTAL RESERVATIONS

As we saw in the previous essay, to lie is to say something deliberately that is contrary to what a person is thinking. Lying, however, is not restricted just to words, since there is also such a thing as nonverbal communication. The important factor is that some other person, who is the intended object of communication, is deceived either by word or deed. Obviously, therefore, a person cannot, strictly speaking, lie to himself.

There are many different kinds of communication, so it is important to be aware of the mode of discourse in each instance before accusing someone of lying. Thus, a joke is not a lie when it is obvious that the mode of discourse is joking. When Bob Hope points out the foibles of our politicians with a series of one-liners, he is not lying. A father telling fairy tales to his young daughter is not lying, for the normal child instinctively senses the difference between a "story" and her everyday life. Writers of fiction, script writers for films and television programs are not lying, since the normal person recognizes immediately that they are operating in the realm of imagination.

The liar must say something that is in opposition to what he knows to be true. Thus it is a lie actually to tell the truth when one thinks that he is saying something false. On the other hand it is not a lie to say what is actually false when one thinks it is true. We all err in this latter way, since often what we think is true turns out to be false. This is due to our limitations, our weakness and our ignorance.

Since lying is contrary to the natural moral law, it is never allowed. Thus, a deliberate lie is always a sin—something that is contrary to the will of God and his law for us. In itself a lie, though intrinsically evil, is a venial sin. However, lying becomes mortally sinful if another virtue besides veracity (for example, justice or charity) is thereby gravely violated. Accordingly, it is a mortal sin to tell a lie under oath or to deny one's Catholic faith.

Even though we may never tell a lie, there are times when we are bound in conscience to conceal the truth. For we are not obliged at all times to tell the whole truth. The reason for this is that secrets must be kept, and the good reputation of another can be ruined by revealing what is true about him but should not be made known. Often silence is the best policy, but this is not always possible, especially when one is asked specific questions.

Thus we are sometimes confronted with a real moral dilemma: as the result of direct questioning we find ourselves in a situation of being obliged both to veil the truth and to speak the truth. How does one escape without sinning? The best known solution to the dilemma is what is called a "mental reservation", which may be of two kinds. In both cases the speaker limits the accepted sense of his words to a particular meaning. To limit the meaning and give no clue is called a *strict mental reservation*. If one limits the meaning of the answer and leaves a reasonable clue to the sense intended, it is called by the moralists a *broad mental reservation*.

A strict mental reservation is nothing but a lie and therefore is sinful. It is used when the actual meaning of the statement can in no way be inferred from the external circumstances. An example would be the case of one who says, "I have not stolen anything"—and adds mentally to himself only—"with the left hand, but with the right".

A broad mental reservation is had if the real meaning of the expression can be inferred either from the circumstances of the question, or from customary usage, even if, as a matter of fact, such inference is not actually made. Thus, in answering the telephone or the door, to say that someone is not at home or "is not in" leaves open the reasonable inference that the person is physically there but not available.

Broad mental reservations are often used in business and social communication. They are morally permissible, sometimes even obligatory, provided there is a sufficient reason for using them and the questioner has no real right to know the truth. A sufficient reason would be the safeguarding of anything necessary for body or soul or the evading of annoying and unreasonable questions. However, if the one asking the question has a right to the full answer, such as a parent or superior or official, then the broad mental reservation may not be used. One must utter the full truth.

If officials are asked about matters of professional secrecy by persons without authority they may answer "I do not know," that is, "anything that I may communicate." This applies even more to priests when they are asked about matters pertaining to confession.

From a moral point of view, great care should be used in employing mental reservations. Human speech is supposed to communicate the truth—it is not supposed to be a puzzle. Truth builds up community, while lies and obfuscations tend to destroy it. So one should not lightly resort to the mental reservation.

I once had a friend who constantly used mental reservations in normal conversation. Everyone knew it. The result was that his friends tended to discount all he said, since they could not be sure whether he was telling the truth or offering some "hidden meaning".

Truth is always the best policy and we should not veil it unless we really have sufficient reason to do so.

51

ON KEEPING SECRETS

An important part of observing the Eighth Commandment, "You shall not bear false witness against your neighbor," is keeping secrets. What do we mean by a "secret"? A secret is the knowledge of some thing which may not be revealed, for example, an invention, a hidden sin or some fact—such as the financial embarrassment of a friend.

Traditionally, moralists distinguish three types of secrets, each of which has its own level of confidentiality. The three types of secrets are: natural, promised and entrusted (or committed).

Natural secrets are those which must be kept by reason of the natural law. Common sense tells most people that secrets of this type may not be revealed. These include things that I might know about another person because of what I have seen or heard or perhaps even been told by him. We can recognize these secrets, which are very common, by asking ourselves if we would want such information about ourselves revealed by someone else.

Promised secrets are those which a person has promised to keep after having come across some confidential information. The main idea behind such secrets is that the knowledge is first gained and then the person whom it concerns asks me not to reveal it—and I promise to keep the secret.

Entrusted (or committed) *secrets* are those that depend on an agreement made before the hidden knowledge has been communicated. Such agreements can be either implicit or explicit. Professional secrets of all kinds belong to this category, such as the confidential information confided to doctors, lawyers, counsellors, psychiatrists and so forth. Information and sins communicated to a priest in the course of sacramental confession belong to this class of secrets, though the obligation to silence which binds him is much more strict than that which binds others.

Why must secrets be kept? Or, to put it another way, why is it sinful to reveal hidden information about another person? The fundamental reason is that each person has a natural right to that which belongs to him, whether it is real property or an idea or an invention. He also has a natural right to his good reputation. Each person in his own way is creative and has a right to the fruits of his efforts. Thus each person has his own secrets which belong to him and may not be taken away, unless more weighty reasons of justice and charity intervene.

When is one morally justified in revealing a secret? The obligation to keep a secret varies, depending on the type of secret involved. Thus, it is a grave sin against justice or charity to violate a natural secret, if the person involved is seriously injured or deeply offended by the revelation. A sufficient reason for revealing such secrets is the threat of great harm to another or to the Church or to the state.

The obligation to keep a promised secret depends on how seriously the one who made the promise intended to bind himself. Unless the obligation was made binding explicitly under serious sin, it would bind only venially. A sufficient reason for revealing a promised secret is any great inconvenience to oneself in keeping it, unless one has promised to keep it despite such inconvenience.

Entrusted secrets are the most binding because of the nature of the confidentiality involved. Their revelation would cause great harm to society. For, the common good requires that professional people receive and keep confidential information. If secret information communicated to doctors and lawyers were easily made public, then people would not go to them and this would cause great injury to society. There are, however, certain extreme circumstances that can justify the revelation to the proper authorities of entrusted secrets, for example, in order to ward off great imminent danger to some innocent third party, to the Church or to the state. Thus, if someone is told in confidence that a third party will be murdered, he not only may but he must warn that person of the danger. In general we can say that if an entrusted secret involves a serious violation of justice to other innocent parties, then the obligation to keep the secret ceases. But under no circumstances, even the threat of death, may a priest reveal what he has heard in confession.

What about reading another person's letters or diaries? If such materials are hidden away, it would be sinful to read them unless permission has been given or unless it can reasonably be presumed. This of course does not apply to parents reading the mail of their minor children, especially if they have reason to believe that the letters contain material that might be injurious to the child or the family.

52

CALUMNY AND DETRACTION

One of the main reasons why lies are forbidden by the Eighth Commandment is that they destroy community and healthy social relationships. Since man is a social being he absolutely needs human society in order to grow to full maturity as a man. Consequently, whatever militates against human community is contrary to man's nature, contrary to the will of God and therefore forbidden by God.

Obviously, there are different kinds of lies. "Lies of convenience", that is, lies told in order to extricate oneself from an embarrassing situation, normally do not damage the reputation of another. If successful, they are known only in the depths of the conscience of the one who told them. There are different kinds of statements that injure the reputation of another.

It is possible to injure another's good name either by telling lies about that person or by revealing hidden faults which should not be revealed. To tell lies about another person is called *calumny* or slander. To reveal the hidden faults or sins of another without sufficient cause, in such wise that the person's reputation or good name is seriously damaged, is called the sin of *detraction*. Many people find it hard to remember the exact meaning of each of these words. Years ago one of my grade school teachers, a Franciscan nun, told me that the way to remember which is which is to concentrate on the *l* and the *t*. If you remember that *l* stands for "lie" and *t* stands for "truth", you can recall the difference between calumny and detraction.

I do not believe that it is necessary to belabor the point that each person has a right to his or her good name. A good name is something that we earn by reason of our good deeds. It concerns the public estimation of a person's intellectual and moral excellence. In a very real sense, a person's good name is his or her property—it belongs to the person concerned as a strict right. Hence the violation of a person's good name is a sin against the virtue of justice.

The good name or reputation of another can be damaged, or even totally destroyed, in a number of ways. To calumniate another is certainly to ruin his good name and so to do him an injustice. Many Catholics seem to be unaware of the fact that detraction is also a sin—a sin contrary to the Eighth Commandment. The seriousness of the sin, in the case of both calumny and detraction, depends upon the gravity of the injury done to the other party. The sin can be either venial or mortal, depending on the circumstances.

While treating of the Seventh Commandment, I pointed out that the sins against justice require some kind of *restitution*. It is often hard to determine, in a given case, how this is to be done and how much restitution is required, but the basic principle stands. It follows then, since both calumny and detraction are violations of justice, that both demand some kind of restitution. A person who has lied about another can often right the wrong he has done by retracting the lie and stating the truth. In the case of detraction the situation is more difficult, since it is not a matter of lying but of revealing the hidden sins or faults of another that should not be revealed in these circumstances. Frequently little can be done in the practical order. One cannot deny the statements since they actually are true; to deny them would be to add a lie to the previous detraction. Some moralists recommend, in this situation, apologies and praise of the person's good points.

Do you know what a *rash judgment* is? It is an internal act of the mind by which one person attributes evil actions or motives to another without any kind of evidence for such a judgment. A rash judgment is a kind of lie to oneself. Such judgments damage another person in our own eyes, when there is no really objective reason for doing so. Because of our fallen human nature we all tend to make rash judgments about others—often without even reflecting on what we are doing. It is especially easy to judge rashly people we do not like, people who have offended us, people who differ from us in one way or another. It is unreasonable to make rash judgments. Such judgments involve a misuse of our interior faculties, especially our mind and our will. Hence they are contrary to the Eighth Commandment and sinful. We should examine ourselves to see if we occasionally rashly judge others and we should strive to make our judgments correspond to the facts.

What is in our minds is eventually uttered by our tongues. The tongue is a small member of the body, but it possesses great power—either for good or for evil.

53

TRUTH AND THE MEDIA

My treatment of the Eighth Commandment will conclude with a few observations on the communications media. The moral obligation to speak the truth applies to newspaper reporters, columnists, radio and television announcers just as much as it applies to the individual in his or her personal relationships with others.

God created man with an intelligence or mind that naturally seeks the truth. The desire of the human mind for truth is just as strong as the urge of the hungry man for food or the need of the fish for water. Thus man has a natural right to the truth and since he is a social being and lives in society it follows that society also has a right to truthful information. If that is true for all men, it is especially so in a free society such as a democracy, since the citizens need accurate, reasonably complete information in order to vote wisely and fulfill their civic duties.

For every right there is also a corresponding duty. This means in the present context that those who manage and conduct the media in our society have a very serious obligation to keep the people well informed, especially in those matters of greater concern to the well-being of society. Above all, they must tell the truth to the best of their ability. Also, in selecting what to report and what to omit out of the vast amount of information available each day they must keep in mind the common good rather than some short-term gain for a favored group or individual.

The right to information, however, like all human rights, is not absolutely unlimited, since it can come into conflict with other and higher rights of others. Thus, in some cases the right of privacy and the right of secrecy of individuals or groups will require that some "news" be either totally suppressed or delayed to a more opportune time. The validity of such limitations on the right to know is obvious to all in crisis situations, such as terrorist highjackings, when, if certain confidential information were leaked to the press, the lives of hundreds of people would be endangered.

The traditional understanding of the Eighth Commandment saw it directed almost exclusively to the speaker or communicator. In our day, when there is so much communication, news and entertainment available via press, radio and television on a 24-hour a day basis, new dimensions of the Commandment can be discerned. Thus, responsibility for truth and accuracy in the media falls not just on the authors but also on the "consumers"—on those who read, listen and watch.

In a certain sense we should all be "watchdogs" for errors, abuses and distortions in the media. Much can be done to maintain high standards in the media if the "recipients" write letters, telephone and in general let the communicators know what they think of their performance. Many people do not seem to realize it, but letters to the editor, for example, can often have much influence on business and public officials.

The Eighth Commandment also concerns our use of the media. Moderation is to be striven for in all dimensions of human living. This is certainly true of our use of the mass media. Many people waste precious hours reading, listening to or watching useless trash. The evidence seems to be mounting that excessive television viewing on the part of American children is contributing to the steady decline in academic performance. By its very nature television watching is mostly passive. In the area of creativity in children, there is a big difference between watching a television show and playing games. I am reminded here of a family I once visited in Vancouver, B.C. They had two teenage daughters. They did not spend very much time looking at television, but when they did it was to see a particular program that had been carefully selected in advance. After the program, the set was turned off and they would then discuss the show, asking such questions as: What idea was the show trying to convey? what were the unstated assumptions? did they achieve their objective? was the program successful?

After a lifetime of such critical reflection and judgment, you can just imagine how sharp those girls must have been. I conversed with them for a few hours and can testify that they were very critical and very intelligent. In that case, the family dominated the media instead of being a slave to them.

There is immense power for good and evil in the mass media today. We Catholics should be aware of that power and do what we can to influence it in the direction of truth and completeness.

54

ON AVOIDING
EVIL THOUGHTS AND DESIRES

The last two Commandments are directed to man's mind and heart, that is, they concern the interior life of each person where thoughts and desires reign supreme. Thus, God's law touches not just the exterior act but also the interior dimension of thinking and willing. Obviously, the Ninth Commandment is closely linked with the Sixth, and the Tenth Commandment relates to the Seventh.

The Ninth Commandment is found in Deuteronomy (5:21): "You shall not covet your neighbor's wife." The word "covet" means: to wish for enviously, to desire inordinately or culpably. Thus, the Ninth Commandment tells us to be pure in thought and desire and it forbids all thoughts and desires contrary to the virtue of chastity.

On numerous occasions Jesus warned his disciples to

avoid all unclean and wicked desires. One of the eight beatitudes covers this matter: "Blessed are the clean of heart, for they shall see God" (Mt 5:8). In another place Jesus says: "For out of the heart come evil thoughts, murders, adulteries, immorality, thefts, false witness, blasphemies. These are the things that defile a man" (Mt 15:19–20).

St. Paul stressed the same idea: "Therefore mortify your members, which are on earth: immorality, uncleanness, lust, evil desire and covetousness (which is a form of idol-worship). Because of these things the wrath of God comes upon the unbelievers" (Col 3:5–6). And St. Peter warns us in his first letter: "Beloved, I exhort you as strangers and pilgrims to abstain from carnal desires which war against the soul" (2:11).

Some Catholics seem to think that only external acts are sinful and that the law of God does not govern one's inner thoughts and desires. The above quotations from Scripture should show very clearly that that idea is erroneous. However, a careful distinction should be made between evil thoughts that are spontaneous, unprovoked and unwilled and those that are deliberately willed and fostered. A sign of our fallen nature—that some of the effects of original sin are still with us—is that we do not have complete control over our thoughts and desires. Sometimes evil thoughts come into our minds and we do not know where they come from or why—ideas of hatred or revenge, adulterous thoughts, impure desires, even blasphemous thoughts. It is very important to remember that such thoughts, no matter how evil or how persistent they might be, are not sinful as long as one does not give consent to them. When tormented by such thoughts we should have immediate recourse to prayer and also divert our attention to other good or harmless objects. This is the advice that the masters of the spiritual life have given for centuries.

Thus, thoughts about impure things become sinful when a person thinks of an unchaste act and deliberately takes pleasure in so thinking, or when unchaste desire or passion is aroused and consent is given to it. It should be clear, then, that pornography in all of its forms, since its purpose is to stimulate lustful desires and passions, is condemned and forbidden by the Ninth Commandment.

The Tenth Commandment is: "You shall not covet your neighbor's goods" (Dt 5:21). God's Tenth "Word" or Commandment applies the notion of "covetousness" to the realm of material possessions. It forbids all willful desire to take or to keep unjustly what belongs to others, and it also forbids envy at their success. Please note that the Commandment covers such desires that are deliberately willed or fostered. If a person suddenly realizes that he is beset by such thoughts but has not deliberately consented to them, then there is no sin. Sin enters into the picture when one comes to the full realization of what one is doing, knows that it is sinful, but then deliberately persists in that activity. You may break one of God's laws at times without knowing it but that is not the same thing as committing a sin. You cannot commit a sin by chance or by accident or by not knowing what you are doing.

Scripture also warns us against greed: "Take heed and guard yourselves from all covetousness, for a man's life does not consist in the abundance of his possessions" (Lk 12:15). And again: "For covetousness is the root of all evils, and some in their eagerness to get rich have strayed from the faith and have involved themselves in many troubles" (1 Tim 6:10).

By means of his Ninth and Tenth Commandments the Lord is telling us to avoid all evil desires. This does not mean that our minds should be a vacuum. On the contrary. We should cultivate good and holy and healthy desires. If we do that consistently then we will be rewarded with both spiritual and psychological health.